TRAINING THEORY

By

FRANK W. DICK O.B.E.

(Director of Coaching)

© BRITISH AMATEUR ATHLETIC BOARD

Edgbaston House, 3 Duchess Place, Birmingham B16 8NM

About the Author

FRANK DICK O.B.E., B.Sc., D.L.C., F.B.I.S.C., is the B.A.A.B's Director of Coaching; President of the European Athletics Coaches' Association; Chairman of the British Olympic Association Coaches' Advisory Group. He studied at Edinburgh University, Loughborough, and the University of Oregon, and is a former Fulbright scholar. Applied Biomechanics and the Physiology of Exercise are his specialist fields, and these combined with his detailed study of training methods have established him as Britain's foremost authority in Training Theory and in the synthesis of sports science for coaches.

An international athlete himself, he has, whilst specialising in sprints, coached athletes to medals at Commonwealth and Olympic Games and at European and World Championships. He has been responsible for Britain's relay teams since 1978, and has been Director of Coaching and Chief Coach for the National Team since 1979.

Author's Acknowledgements

This booklet owes its substance to everyone with whom I have come in contact as a coach and as a teacher. I am particularly indebted to the following:—

The athletes from several sports I have had the privilege to coach for helping me link theory and practice.

My National Coaching colleagues and fellow coaches for their expertise and for their interpretation of training theory.

Dunfermline College of Physical Education for access to their excellent library, and for contribution to content via academic staff.

The Scottish International Education Trust for enabling me to attend international conferences to hear the interpretation of training theory in other countries.

The British Amateur Athletic Board for supporting the introduction of this book to the range already available.

My former secretaries, Janet Leyland; Diane Bates; and present secretary Melanie Jones for their many hours of translating the world's worst writing.

To all — I extend my most sincere gratitude.

Cover photograph of Peter Elliott by Mark Shearman

Contents

First edition 1978
Second edition 1984
This edition 1991

Designed, typeset in Times Roman and printed on 115gsm Fineblade Cartridge by Reedprint Ltd, Windsor, Berkshire, England.

ISBN   0 85134 058 X   3M/11M/3/91

Introduction

Athletics, like many other activities ranging from ballet to karate, provides for those who train for, and contest, one or several of its many events or disciplines, an opportunity to express their personalities physically. Unlike swimming or skiing, it has very little appeal at a recreational level, because its nature requires considerable commitment of time and of energy in pursuit of those objectives which define success or excellence in this competitive sport. Nevertheless, it is practised by both sexes and by a very wide age range – a fact underlined by popular growth of "age group" and "vets" athletics. While sports such as gymnastics and figure skating are subjectively judged, athletics provides objective measurement against the stop watch and the metre tape. Technical excellence cannot, however, be considered as solely the prerogative of the more obviously "aesthetic" sports. The athlete must improve and channel his energy systems through a developing technique, or series of techniques, in pursuit of the CITIUS, ALTIUS, FORTIUS theme. Consequently, the sport affords two separate challenges:—

Striving to improve
(challenging oneself)

or the concept of the pursuit of excellence or success, the measure of which is an improvement of a "personal best" time, height or distance. The award schemes (e.g. Five Star, Thistle) are examples of schemes based on this concept.

Striving to win
(challenging others)

or the concept of the pursuit of absolute excellence or success, the measure of which is in beating an opponent. Club competitions and individual championships are examples of this type of challenge.

To meet these objectives, which might be summarised as pursuit of competitive advantage, the athlete requires

Lifestyle Management — Personal development in its broadest context
Performance Management — All aspects related to preparation and competition
Medical Management — Injury prevention, diagnosis and treatment; medical monitoring.

The coach directs the athlete's commitment to meeting these objectives, and although management and competition are the more direct responsibility of other agencies (e.g. club, association), he must ensure fulfilment of these requirements. This is a sizeable undertaking, because it demands a knowledge of all aspects of the athlete's life and of the environment about him. The athlete takes the challenge of his objectives (his means of expressing himself) very seriously and, in according the coach the honour of directing such expression, the athlete is also requesting acceptance of a great responsibility. The coach's task, then, is varied and complex – and some facets are worth highlighting here.

The coach has a teaching role when helping the athlete learn the techniques required of an event or events. These must be presented on the basis of a thorough understanding of technique, because faults developed in the learning stages are extremely difficult to correct later. The coach is also instrumental in the athlete learning rules, use of equipment, safety, prevention of injury and so on.

4

From the coach, the athlete will learn the practical import of fitness, of training, of exercises and of schedules (microcycles). These will grow into the disciplines of training and of commitment to pursuing short and long term programmes. The athlete should also understand procedure in the event of injury or illness. It is essential, then, that the coach understands all relevant areas of training theory.

The athlete will develop many attitudes through his work with a coach. For example, there are attitudes to sport in general and to athletics in particular; to athletes, officials, coaches and administrators; to National Associations; to the club, and other clubs; to rules and regulations; and so on. Broadly speaking these attitudes should be born of a healthy respect for – and recognition of – the various roles, talents, values and codes which are associated with these persons and agencies. They must never reflect malice, prejudice, discourtesy or "rule bending", because such will blind the athlete from his real objectives relative to athletics. Related to this area is the establishing of those ethics and mores governing the relationship between coach and athlete, coach and coach, and coach and administration.

The possible transfer of these attitudes and of the underlying philosophies of sport to life in general is hardly a new concept. However, it is difficult to say to what extent this may occur without areas of transfer being pointed out to the athlete. Because of the position of athletics in the athlete's life, and because of the considerable contact time between athlete and coach, the coach must consider his broader education role in this respect.

The coach is also an adviser on the many health-, fitness-, sport-related areas. The athlete will learn from the coach such things as essential hygiene, correct nutrition, the value of clean air and sunlight, and the need for adequate sleep. He will also learn to manage his day to day routine of living via the balance of work, study, relaxation and training. Moreover, he will learn the need to share problems in order to keep his life as free as possible from unnecessary stress. This said, the coach is frequently the athlete's confidant. The athlete will seek advice on problems far removed from sport. He will develop an unshakeable loyalty and even an unquestioning trust. To the coach the athlete will turn to share the joy of success – and understanding in failure. No situation involving coach-athlete contact should pass without the coach using it to the athlete's general or specific educational benefit. For example, although there is a very clear rule concerning the use of drugs in sport, athletes may seek clarification on its wording or interpretation. The coach has a responsibility at that point to emphasise the fact that he does not condone the use of drugs; to ensure that the athlete understands what has gone into making the rule; and to taking all available measures to encourage the athlete to obey the rule.

The coach is a creator – never a destroyer – even though an athlete's personality seems so strong that it is tempting to "bring him down" in order to contain him within a dimension that the coach can control. The coach must expand to accommodate the athlete; the athlete must never be made to contract to be accommodated. In other words, as a creator the coach is not like a sculptor chipping at stone until it assumes the shape he seeks; he is like a gardener who works with *living* things. He helps them grow naturally towards perfection – pruning, binding, nourishing – and constantly aware that the plant must be allowed to grow. The coach must be especially aware of this when working in the dynamic situation of coaching the young athlete.

5

Although the athlete has the fundamental motivation to pursue the objectives of improved performance and/or competitive advantage, it is initially the coach who is chiefly responsible for forging the link between training and pursuit of these objectives. At this stage, the athlete derives considerable motivation to train from the coach. In fact, some young athletes want success for the *coach*! However, it is the athlete who must eventually be his own chief motivator and have his own discipline to succeed. The coach should work towards giving the athlete independence, and to changing the situation from one of being the athlete's source of inspiration to one of reflecting the athlete's own inspiration.

Today's coach in athletics must, then, fulfil many functions for the athlete – and must constantly update his knowledge of the dynamic human "material" with which he works; of the relevance of the athlete's total environment to his athletics; of the technical developments in a given event; and of the contribution of related sciences to the development of sport. It is against this backcloth that this training theory booklet has been prepared.

Chapter 1

A day in the life . . . *(The Athlete's Total Environment)*

Athletics is only one part of the athlete's lifestyle. This chapter should serve as a "window" to those aspects which influence his involvement in the sport.

It is well established that regular physical activity is essential to normal growth and a healthful life. Nevertheless it is far from being accepted that a period should be set aside each day for exercise. Consequently, the athlete requires guidance in structuring his daily routine to accommodate training time within a pattern of study/occupation, recreation, eating, basic necessities of personal hygiene and sleep (figure 1). Weekends normally see a greater freedom in terms of training time.

Figure 1.
Possible breakdown of the athlete's day

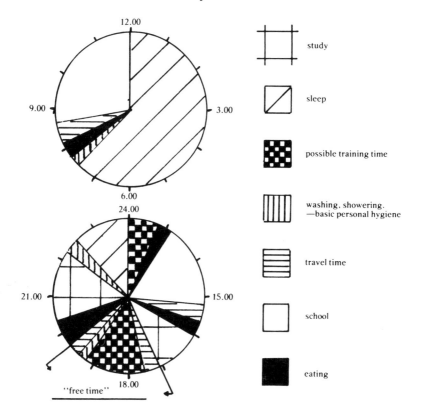

7

Study/occupation
In the total scheme of things, study and/or occupation hold a higher priority status than does athletics training. When individual circumstances add stress to the basic energy costs (table 1a) of this aspect of the athlete's lifestyle, it is clear that the athlete's training capacity and performance will be reduced. In planning training, this should be borne in mind. The physical content of the athlete's life outside athletics; school/university/professional examinations and the study period leading up to them; threatened unemployment and its financial implications; irregular working hours or the need to change work/study venues from time to time; changing patterns of physical work, as for example in moving from school to Physical Education College; these are all examples of factors which must be considered under this heading.

TABLE 1a
Energy expenditure of various occupations (from ASTRAND and RODAHL) based on average man (70kg) and average woman (55kg)

	OCCUPATION	AVERAGE DAILY ENERGY EXPENDITURE (K.Cals)
MEN	Office worker	2520
	Laboratory technician	2840
	University student	2930
	Building worker	3000
	Farmer	3550
WOMEN	Laboratory technician	2130
	Assistant in department store	2250
	University student	2290
	Factory worker	2320
	Bakery worker	2510

Recreation
For many athletes, athletics is their only recreation. For others, a wide range of physical recreation, cultural pursuits and so on on the one hand, and social interests such as girl friends/boy friends on the other, take a proportion of the athlete's time, energy and pocket money. It is worth pointing out that each of the latter may influence the athlete's involvement in athletics. For example, if the involvement with girl friend/boy friend is time consuming, less time is available to train; if the recreation is intensely physical, less energy is left for training; and if the cultural pursuit is costly, depending on his means, the athlete may find it very difficult to do athletics *and* the cultural interest. In short, value judgements are involved; they are the athlete's to make, and the athlete should be objectively advised in his evaluation of recreation/interest against athletics in terms of priority and commitment, and in the allocation of time, energy and cost accordingly.

Eating
Regular meals providing the correct quantity and quality of nutrition demanded by the athlete's lifestyle are essential to his total well-being.

Regularity of meal times is an important discipline to ensure time for relaxed digestion of appropriate nutritional requirements. Should circumstances cause departure from the established routine of meal times, the athlete must allow at least two hours to elapse between meal and training/competition.

There is normally little problem in encouraging the athlete to eat sufficient *quantity* of food. The quantity might be thought of as the energy intake or calorific value of the diet. Ideally, this should equate with the energy cost or calorific output of the athlete's lifestyle (table 1b). This can be calculated from the equation: Daily energy expenditure = time spent in each activity (mins) × metabolic cost of the activity. (Kcals/min) based on average man/woman.

TABLE 1b
Energy cost of various physical activities (various sources)

ACTIVITY	AVERAGE ENERGY COST (K.Cals/min)
Cross Country	10–20
Playing squash	10–20
Playing tennis	7–10
Playing football	9
Running (3:45.0/km)	19–20
Circuit training	12

If input be greater than output, the athlete will gain weight; and should this be the case, the athlete should reduce his intake of calories from carbohydrates (e.g. pastries, cakes, sweets, etc.) and fats (e.g. cooking oils, butter, etc.) whilst maintaining his intake of proteins, vitamins and minerals. Severe weight problems require medical advice.

It is the *quality* of the athlete's diet that gives cause for most concern. An adequate calorific value of food intake via carbohydrates and fats will certainly make available the necessary fuels for physical activity, but would not supply the vital materials for maintenance, repair and the running of the body's various systems. The athlete must therefore be assured of:—

a daily protein intake of 1-2gm per kg body weight (meat, cheese, fish, etc.). (See Table 2a).
a distribution of calorific intake of 50% from carbohydrates, 40% from fats and 10% from proteins.
a daily supplement of water soluble vitamins (vitamins C and B complex) (e.g. 1gm effervescent Redoxon Ascorbic Acid plus 1 tablet BC500). (See Table 2b).
*an occasional supplement of fat soluble vitamins (vitamins A, D, E and K) (e.g. multivitamin tablets such as Plurivite, Supavite, etc.).
*an occasional supplement of minerals (e.g. iron, phosphorous, calcium tablets), and salts (e.g. in Sportive Perform Mineral +6).

*Medical advice on the most suitable preparations for individual athletes should be obtained.

Although many special preparations such as pollen tablets and Biostrath are well documented as to their value and safety, the athlete should be discouraged from experimentation with new preparations without guidance from authorities in medicine or nutritional physiology. Alcohol and tobacco are quite definitely "out" for athletes.

Western eating habits and the refined nature of foods have led to a relatively low "roughage" content in the diet. "Roughage" is that indigestible portion of foods which ensures the steady passage of foods through the digestive tract, keeping the athlete "regular". Bran-type cereals for breakfast are therefore recommended.

9

TABLE 2a
PROTEIN NEEDS AND BODYWEIGHT

Athletes need to ensure adequate protein intake. Supplementing the diet with one of the several proprietary brand protein powders will meet most athletes' requirements.

Body Weight (kg)	Daily Protein Need (2g/kg)	Protein Intake: Regular Diet (g)	Additional Protein Need (g/day)	alternative way to meet your additional need:
55	110	90	20	* 2 tablespoons of Protein Powder
60	120	90	30	* 3 tablespoons of Protein Powder
65	130	90	40	* 4 tablespoons of Protein Powder
70	140	90	50	* 5 tablespoons of Protein Powder
75	150	90	60	* 6 tablespoons of Protein Powder
80	160	100	60	* 6 tablespoons of Protein Powder
85	170	110	60	* 6 tablespoons of Protein Powder
90	180	110	70	* 7 tablespoons of Protein Powder
95	190	120	70	* 7 tablespoons of Protein Powder

* Protein Powder: 1 dessertspoon is about 6g; 1 tablespoon is about 10g.

Reproduced by courtesy of Wandor Food's Research Unit.

TABLE 2b

Daily vitamin intake recommended by G.D.R. physiologists GÖTTE and SCHNEIDER

VITAMIN	ENDURANCE ACTIVITY (mg)	ELASTIC STRENGTH ACTIVITY (mg)
A	4–5	4–5
B_1	6–8	6–8
B_2	6–8	8–12
B_6	6–8	10–15
B_{12}	5–6µg	5–6µg
Niacin	20–30	30–40
C	400–800	300–500

Training

Training content is dealt with in separate chapters, and comment here is restricted to considering those aspects of the athlete's environment which influence training.

The athletics environment

In order to derive maximum value from training, the athlete requires access to relevant *facilities* and *equipment* (Table 3). Limited access—or the absence of certain facilities/equipment—in obliging the athlete to compromise his training programme, implies reduced training effect and prejudices the athlete's development.

Ideally, *coaching* should be available for all training units. Technical work requires constant supervision; high intensity endurance loads require motivation to overcome pain and fear; many training units require management, either for basic organisation or for safety; and all training requires evaluation. Moreover, having a coach available for technical discussion, and as a companion, makes training more palatable!

TABLE 3
Facilities and equipment for training

The coach may be confronted by a wide ranging quality of facility and equipment. Nevertheless he must use whatever exists to the athlete's advantage. Some of the range of situations are listed here.

SPECIALIST	GENERAL
International specification stadia —outdoor and indoor	Woodland and open country
	Parks and race courses, sports fields
Indoor training halls	Beaches—surf and dunes
Outdoor training areas	Roads—lanes—paths
Fully equipped strength training rooms	Assembly halls
Fully equipped gymnasia or sports halls	Air halls, swimming pools
International specification equipment— outdoor and indoor	Logs, cabers, stones, tyres
Sling balls, varied throwing weights, medicine balls	Steps, walls, fences
Throwing nets, harnesses, weighted jackets	Rope, elastic, pulleys
Starzynski boards, benches, boxes, wallbars, beams	Dividing nets, golf nets, cricket nets
Spring boards, parallel bars, crash mats, trampolines	Heavy boots, weighted vests

Resource materials in the form of articles, books, photo-sequences, video cassettes, films and so on are valuable contributions to the athlete's understanding of his event. These should be available from some central location such as a college, club, sports complex, Department of Recreation and Leisure or Sports Council.

Prevention of injury is not easy in a sport where increasingly high demands are made of an athlete in training and in competition. However, the athlete must be made aware of how to reduce the risk, and the coach has a considerable responsibility in this direction. Consequently, the coach should help the athlete establish certain "codes".

Safety: Each event has its own safety procedures. These must be learned and followed.

Equipment must never be left lying around (e.g. rakes, javelins, barbells, etc.).

Personal and event equipment must always be checked to ensure that it does not represent a safety hazard.

All working surfaces must be consistent with safety.

When many events are being practised in the area a "safe working code" must be established and adhered to.

Health: Ideally, before winter training commences, the athlete should have a medical, physical, physiological and dental check-up.

Following injury or illness, the athlete must be sufficiently disciplined to restrict training to a programme modified by the coach.

11

The athlete should be au fait with matters of basic hygiene.

Should immunisation, vaccination, etc. be necessary, these are best attended to before the winter programme commences—and certainly as far as possible from the competition period.

A regular daily routine such as in figure 1 should be followed.

All daily nutritional requirements should be met.

The spirit and letter of the laws of the sport concerning doping should be adhered to.

The athlete must immediately inform the coach of any changes in basic health status (i.e. injury, illness). The coach will then request the athlete to rest or to work on a modified programme *until basic health status is restored.* NO HEALTH UPSETS, HOWEVER SLIGHT, MUST BE IGNORED.

The athlete should warm up and warm down in each training unit.

Training *must* cease when there are "warning signs" such as sharp pains, muscle twinges and so on.

The coach should, if possible, have a basic knowledge of first aid.

Methodics: The structure of training units is discussed in separate chapters.

Basic physical preparation of strength, endurance and mobility must precede technical development and specific physical preparation (Figure 2).

Poorly learned techniques and/or lack of basic physical preparation constitute fertile ground for future overuse injury.

Incomplete recovery between training units alters the effect of training to the extent that damage rather than benefit will result. The totality of possible stressors in the athlete's life must be kept in mind here, because the same training unit will have a more severe effect if the athlete is already fatigued due to the stressors of occupation.

Excessively biased training represents the probability of disproportionate stress on one or several of the body's systems, and the considerable risk of overuse injury or damage.

Training methods to encourage relaxation should be used from time to time (e.g. autogenic training).

Figure 2.

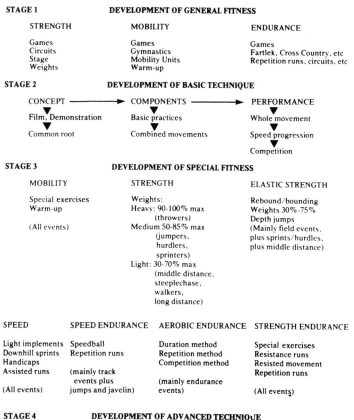

STAGE 1   DEVELOPMENT OF GENERAL FITNESS

STRENGTH	MOBILITY	ENDURANCE
Games	Games	Games
Circuits	Gymnastics	Fartlek, Cross Country, etc
Stage	Mobility Units	Repetition runs, circuits, etc
Weights	Warm-up	

STAGE 2   DEVELOPMENT OF BASIC TECHNIQUE

CONCEPT ⟶ COMPONENTS ⟶ PERFORMANCE

Film, Demonstration   Basic practices   Whole movement

Common root   Combined movements   Speed progression

Competition

STAGE 3   DEVELOPMENT OF SPECIAL FITNESS

MOBILITY	STRENGTH	ELASTIC STRENGTH
Special exercises	Weights:	Rebound/bounding
Warm-up	Heavy: 90-100% max	Weights 30%-75%
	(throwers)	Depth jumps
(All events)	Medium 50-85% max	(Mainly field events,
	(jumpers,	plus sprints/hurdles,
	hurdlers,	plus middle distance)
	sprinters)	
	Light: 30-70% max	
	(middle distance,	
	steeplechase,	
	walkers,	
	long distance)	

SPEED	SPEED ENDURANCE	AEROBIC ENDURANCE	STRENGTH ENDURANCE
Light implements	Speedball	Duration method	Special exercises
Downhill sprints	Repetition runs	Repetition method	Resistance runs
Handicaps		Competition method	Resisted movement
Assisted runs	(mainly track		Repetition runs
	events plus	(mainly endurance	
(All events)	jumps and javelin)	events)	(All events)

STAGE 4   DEVELOPMENT OF ADVANCED TECHNIQUE

Specialised Practices and Drills

An athlete may, however, become injured and/or ill, and he should have access to *medical* and *paramedical back-up*. Rapid diagnosis and treatment of injury or illness is extremely important to the athlete, because he wishes to lose the least possible number of training days. This requires teamwork involving the athlete's own G.P. who, hopefully, has some sympathy with the athlete's sense of urgency; a physiotherapist with a knowledge of sports injuries; a physiological testing laboratory; access to a sauna and to massage; and the possibility of a "retreat" to encourage relaxation and accelerate recuperation (e.g. hills, seaside, sunshine).

Most aspects of the athlete's "athletics environment" are covered by the collective efforts of club, institution (e.g. school, college, university, services), association, Board, local government Departments of Recreation and Leisure, and so on. (Figure 3). The well organised club will help coordinate and "manage" this area of the athlete's life, but in the absence of this organisation the responsibilty rests with the coach.

13

Figure 3.
The athlete's environment
Athletics is only one part of the athlete's varied and complex environment.

The non-athletics environment

Finance (or rather the limitations it can impose) is possibly the greatest single factor in this area. Food, equipment, entry fees, enrolment fees, travel and so on require a sizeable outlay from the athlete's resources. Of course, it should be said that the sport could be looked upon as the athlete's "hobby" and that the athlete should, therefore, accept that he should pay for it. However, when athletes display progress towards Regional/National level and a deep commitment to progress further, it would harm both athlete and sport if the athlete had to give up his "hobby" due to lack of funds. Every effort should be made, then, to explore possible sources of assistance, such as contributions from local industry; local government grants; club contributory aid-schemes; and contributions in kind (e.g. passes to sports centres, reduced price kit, etc.).

The geographic location of an athlete's home relative to training venue, club, coach, place of work and social interest may make regular training an extremely difficult problem to solve. Finance may, of course, be involved, but travelling time and implied early rise and late return home is another major consideration. The athlete must be given assistance in this direction to make commitment to regular training an attractive proposition.

Under the *cultural* "umbrella" is the total complex of the athlete's inter-relationship with social groupings without and within athletics. The coach must discuss these with the athlete and understand their significance in order to evaluate their influence on his athletic development. Each of the social groupings may or may not express attitudes concerning the athlete's involvement in athletics. If attitudes *are* expressed, they may range from extremely negative to extremely positive.

If no attitudes are expressed, this may represent a positive *or* negative effect on the athlete.

The nett result of this bombardment of social influences is the dynamic aggregate attitude with which the athlete approaches each training unit, and the sport as a whole (Figure 4). Certain cultural factors have very practical significance. For example, the athlete's religious beliefs may not permit physical exercise on certain days of the week. In order to safeguard the athlete's peace of mind, the coach *must* take this into account in programme construction.

Figure 4.

Many agencies influence the athlete's attitude to athletics.

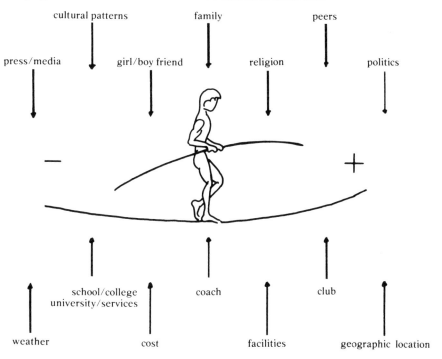

15

Basic necessities of personal hygiene

Very few athletes have to be reminded on points of hygiene because this area of life receives thorough attention at home and at school. However, it is worth drawing the athlete's attention to one or two points of hygiene, applicable to those involved in sport.

Training kit should be regularly laundered.

Towels	— daily.
Underwear and socks	— at least every other day.
Vests and shorts	— at least twice per week.
Sweat tops	— at least once per week.
Tracksuits and wet suits	— at least once per month.

Although it should be understood that no-one should borrow *any* kit from other athletes, it is *definitely forbidden for athletes to borrow towels, underwear or socks.*

Holdalls/kit bags should be completely emptied after *every* training session—and the removed kit should be washed or aired. Wet shoes should be filled with dry paper and allowed to dry out.

The athlete should shower/bathe after every training session and dry himself thoroughly afterwards, especially his feet/toes.

As soon as *any* infection is noticed, e.g. athlete's foot, skin rashes, colds, etc., medical advice should be sought, and the condition treated. Any cuts, scratches or grazes must receive immediate first aid.

Sleep

It is generally accepted that athletes require 8–10 hours sleep per 24 hours. To reduce this time is to reduce the athlete's opportunity to recuperate from the exhausting process of living a very full day.

This broad overview of the background, against which the coach must view his work with the athlete, cannot take stock of all the details which contribute to making every athlete's lifestyle unique. Hopefully it will, however, encourage the coach to be aware that these unique backgrounds have a profound influence on the athlete and on his commitment to athletics.

Chapter 2

. . . I knew him well *(Basic Structure and Function)*

The most basic aims of training might be summarised as
(i) The improved efficiency of energy production (CONDITIONING).
(ii) The improved efficiency of energy expression (TECHNIQUE and CONDITIONING).

ENERGY PRODUCTION

Fuel

The energy required to move limbs is derived from our "fuel". The fuel comes in the first instance from the food we eat. The chief "fuel foods" are *carbohydrates* and *fats* which are broken down to more usable forms by the digestive system to *glucose* (stored as glycogen) and *free fatty acids* respectively. The fuel is carried from the digestive system to storage or circulation by the blood. (Figure 5). It is most unlikely that an athlete will "run out" of fuel. The only possibility would appear to be in the very long endurance runs, e.g. marathon or longer distances.

Occasionally, for personal reasons, athletes (especially girls), go on "diets". These athletes must be observed closely in training for a possible rapid depletion of energy.

Oxygen

Oxygen has a critical role to play in the production of energy from our fuel. The oxygen is transported to the engine (the working muscle) by *Haemoglobin*, the oxygen carrier present in red blood cells. The blood collects its oxygen from the lungs and is pumped by the heart round an elaborate system of blood vessels (arteries, arterioles, capillaries, venules and veins) which link the lungs and the working muscle. The total system is referred to as the OXYGEN TRANSPORTING—or CARDIO RESPIRATORY—or CIRCULO RESPIRATORY— or CARDIO VASCULAR SYSTEM. However, not only does it transport oxygen from lungs to muscle, it also transports waste—the fuel's "ashes"—back to the lungs and excretory systems, to be passed out of the body. (Figure 6).

The heart is obviously a most important agent in this system. Its efficiency is measured by the *Cardiac Output* (C.O.) (the total amount of blood pumped out per minute). This is the product of the *Heart Rate* (H.R.) (the number of beats per minute) and the *Stroke Volume* (S.V.) (the volume of blood pumped with each beat). (Figure 7).

Energy Pathways

The outcome of combusting the fuel is a substance called adenosine tri-phosphate ("Adenosine" plus three "phosphates"), better known by its initials A.T.P. $(A + \overset{+P}{\underset{+P}{}} + P)$. Whenever a "P" is split from the substance, energy is released—the energy which the muscle requires to contract. (Figure 8).

17

Figure 5.

Foods. ▶ to provide energy   for maintenance and repair

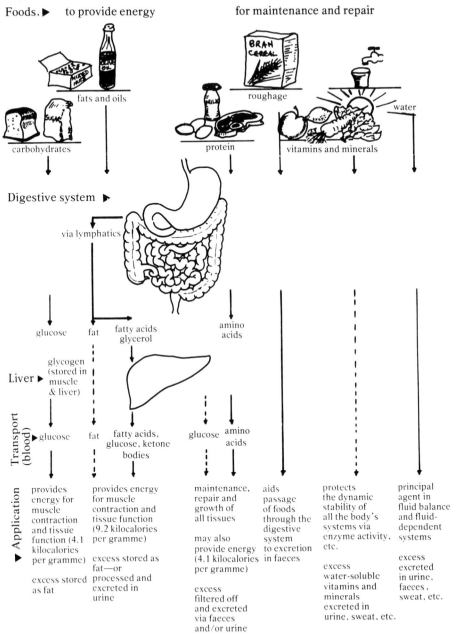

fats and oils   roughage   water

carbohydrates   protein   vitamins and minerals

Digestive system ▶

via lymphatics

glucose   fat   fatty acids glycerol   amino acids

Liver ▶ glycogen (stored in muscle & liver)

Transport (blood) ▶ glucose   fat   fatty acids, glucose, ketone bodies   glucose   amino acids

▶ Application

| provides energy for muscle contraction and tissue function (4.1 kilocalories per gramme)

excess stored as fat | provides energy for muscle contraction and tissue function (9.2 kilocalories per gramme)

excess stored as fat—or processed and excreted in urine | maintenance, repair and growth of all tissues

may also provide energy (4.1 kilocalories per gramme)

excess filtered off and excreted via faeces and/or urine | aids passage of foods through the digestive system to excretion in faeces | protects the dynamic stability of all the body's systems via enzyme activity, etc.

excess water-soluble vitamins and minerals excreted in urine, sweat, etc. | principal agent in fluid balance and fluid-dependent systems

excess excreted in urine, faeces, sweat, etc. |

18

Figure 6.

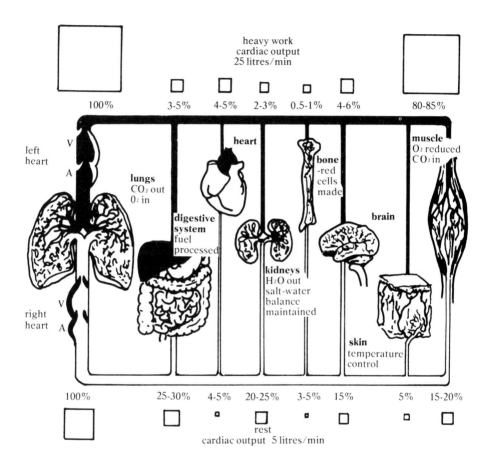

Schematic drawing to show how the small blood vessels are arranged in parallel circuits between arteries (top) and veins (below). Cardiac Output may be increased × 5 when changing from rest to strenuous exercise. The figures indicate the relative distribution of the blood to the various organs at rest (below) and during exercise (above). During exercise, the circulating blood is primarily diverted to the muscles. The area of the squares is proportional to the volume of blood flow per minute.

adapted from original diagram from ASTRAND and RODAHL

19

Figure 7.
$CO = SV \times HR$
Training increases the stroke volume and the range of heart rate.

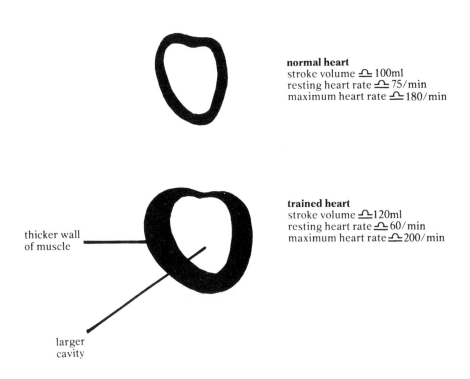

normal heart
stroke volume ≏ 100ml
resting heart rate ≏ 75/min
maximum heart rate ≏ 180/min

trained heart
stroke volume ≏ 120ml
resting heart rate ≏ 60/min
maximum heart rate ≏ 200/min

thicker wall
of muscle

larger
cavity

Figure 8.

$$ATP \longrightarrow ADP + P + ENERGY$$

$$(A + 3P) \longrightarrow (A + 2P) + P + ENERGY$$

ENERGY

+ P   + P
A + P ⟶ A + P
+ P   + P

There are three "pathways" to the production of A.T.P.

1. A fire burns healthily provided there is sufficient oxygen for combustion. The oxygen transporting system can be relied upon to provide sufficient fuel and oxygen for the purposes of muscular activity for as long as the demands of such activity do not exceed the rate at which fuel and oxygen are brought to the muscle. This energy pathway might be summarised as in figure 9, and because this pathway requires oxygen, it is called the AEROBIC ENERGY PATHWAY.

2. Should an athlete work so hard that the body's oxygen requirements exceed the rate of supply, A.T.P. may still be formed, but the waste will accumulate instead of being disposed of. The situation is like the "suffocating" of fire by permitting the ashes to accumulate. The "ashes" in this case is a substance called *lactic acid*. (Figure 9).

Figure 9.

The three energy pathways (adapted from JÄGER and OELSCHLÄGEL)

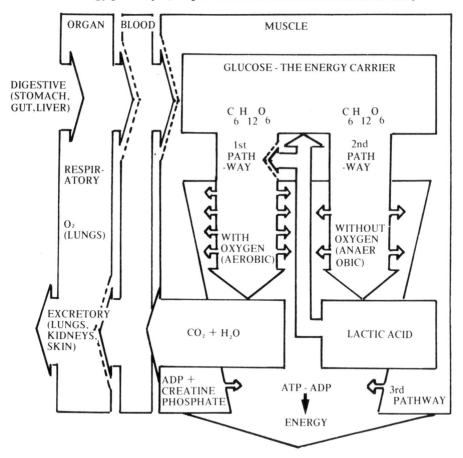

21

Obviously this situation can only last for a limited period of time, after which activity ceases completely and painfully! Time is then required for the lactic acid to be flushed away, and the *oxygen debt*, brought on by attempting to use more than was available, is repaid. This pathway is *without oxygen*, and is therefore called ANAEROBIC. However, because the waste is lactic acid, it is more appropriately referred to as the LACTIC ANAEROBIC PATHWAY. This pathway is exhausted after 45–60 secs of maximal work.

3. Within the muscle itself is a stored energy source—*creatine phosphate*—which might be thought of as a reservoir of phosphate ("P"'s) to replace the "P" when A + 3P's becomes A + 2P's. This replacing process can continue for as long as the "reservoir" lasts—roughly 15 seconds. Again, there is no oxygen—so it is ANAEROBIC—but nor is there any lactic acid; hence this pathway's title of the ALACTIC ANAEROBIC PATHWAY. (Figure 9).

To summarise:—

A.   A.T.P. must be available.

B.   This can be achieved by:

1.   ALACTIC ANAEROBIC PATHWAY (exhausted after 15 seconds).
2.   LACTIC ANAEROBIC PATHWAY   (exhausted after 45–60 seconds).
3.   AEROBIC PATHWAY   (exhausted when fuel runs out, or when the work becomes anaerobic).

The improved efficiency of energy production may only be assumed as an outcome of a well planned training programme provided the body's various "support systems" ensure the general well-being of the athlete. The body consists of a series of organs made up of cells. The health of the cells and consequently of the organs is dependent upon the stable composition of the body's fluids from which the cells obtain nutrition and support for their various functions. The situation might by symbolised as in figure 10. This cycle of dependence will become agitated under the bombardment of *stressors*—and the agitation, a reaction to the stressors,may be thought of as *stress*. The wonderful thing about the body is its ability to *adapt* to stressors so that the stress effect is reduced or eliminated.

Figure 10.
Various factors which may act as stressors to the stability of the body's systems.

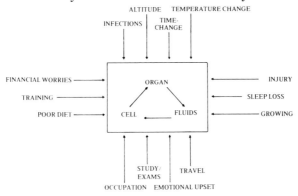

22

Figure 11.
Main bones of the skeletal system.

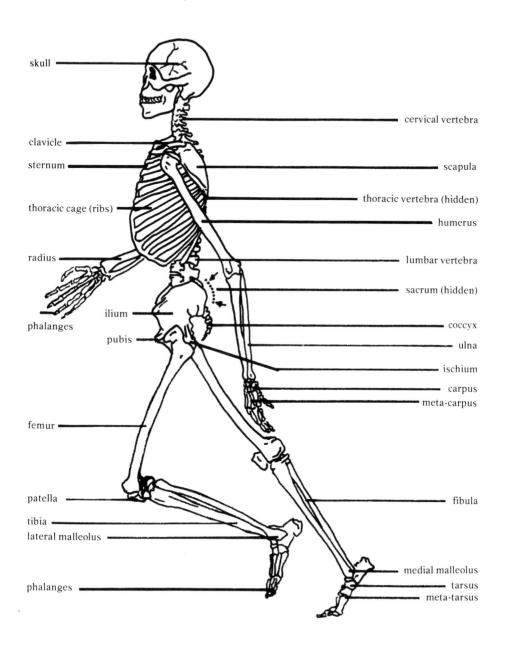

skull

cervical vertebra

clavicle

sternum

scapula

thoracic cage (ribs)

thoracic vertebra (hidden)

humerus

radius

lumbar vertebra

sacrum (hidden)

ilium

phalanges

coccyx

pubis

ulna

ischium

carpus

meta-carpus

femur

patella

fibula

tibia

lateral malleolus

medial malleolus

phalanges

tarsus

meta-tarsus

Carefully programmed training and the thoughtful control of the athlete's environment should ensure a healthy progression of adaptation to training, to the athlete's environment and to the rigours of life outside athletics.

ENERGY EXPRESSION
The athlete's energies are eventually expressed in movement. The principal systems involved in the movement production are:—

(i) The skeletal system.
(ii) The muscular system.
(iii) The central nervous system.

The Skeletal System (Figure 11)
This is the total arrangement of bones, joints, ligaments and cartilage. In the first instance, it is the design of each joint and its supporting ligaments which determines the degree of mobility and stability associated with a given joint. For example, the upper limb complex is designed more for mobility than stability, while the converse is true for the lower limb complex. Some joints have dual functions of equal importance depending on the situation. For example, the spine might be looked upon as a series of joints when mobility is required, but must be seen as a strong "pillar" when stability is sought. Technical problems and even injury risks arise when these functions are confused.

Figure 12.
Main muscle groups in the body.

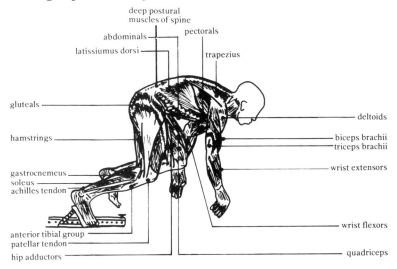

The Muscular System (Figure 12)
It is the pull of muscle on its tendinous attachment to bone that provides the various joint actions. The mechanism involved in effecting that "pull" might be represented by figures 13a and b. When the *contractile component* in the muscle is required to contract, and the energy is provided for the purpose by A.T.P., then the whole muscle shortens—pulling on the *elastic component*—which, in turn, pulls on the bones.

24

Not all muscle contraction actually produces movement. For example, in figure 13c it can be seen that the work of some muscles is *static* while in others it is *dynamic*. Figure 14 shows an athlete whose back muscles are working statically and whose thigh muscles are working dynamically in two ways. In *a* they are forced to *yield* (eccentric muscle contraction) to the body's momentum; while in *c* they are *overcoming* (concentric muscle contraction) the body's weight to propel it from the ground. The yielding action is also referred to as *amortization*, and the point at which yielding changes to overcoming is the *point of amortization*.

Figure 13.

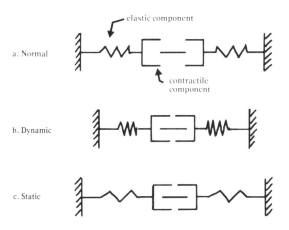

a. Normal

elastic component

contractile component

b. Dynamic

c. Static

Figure 14.

Muscles of back = static work a, b, c.

Thigh muscles of jumping leg = yielding work a, b.

= overcoming work c.

25

Of special interest in sport are those muscles which span two joints. (Figure 15). The efficiency of these muscles relative to a given joint action is completely dependent on the position of a second joint, a critical factor in the development of technique. For example, the position of the hip will dictate the efficiency of the long head of the quadriceps muscle (rectus femoris) as a knee extensor.

Figure 15.

Two joint muscles are the principal agents in postural stability and knowledge of their location is a valuable basis to the understanding of technique.

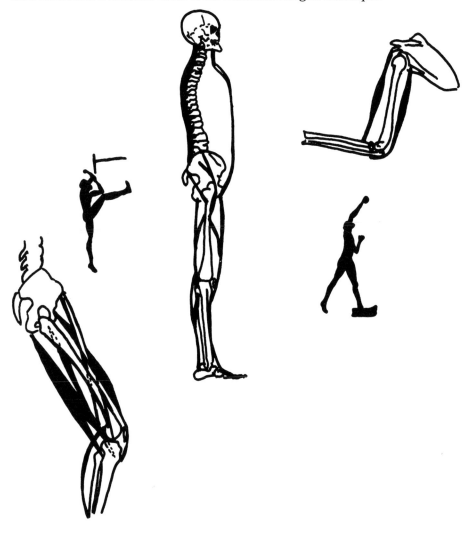

The Central Nervous System
This is the body's own telecommunications network. The pattern of events in the central nervous system might be seen as in figure 16. The brain is seen here as providing the "verb" while the *proprioceptive mechanisms* (feedback systems) provide the "adverb". The final link between the central nervous system and the muscular system is the *motor unit* which is a nerve plus the muscle fibres it supplies. The two systems are frequently referred to collectively as the *neuro-muscular system*. *Reflexes* are mechanisms designed to effect emergency procedures without referal back to "control" (the brain!). These reflexes can, in some instances, be recruited to add to the contributions of the contractile and elastic components of muscle in expressing force and speed of joint action. This is the case, for example, in the *myotonic reflex*, where the sudden forced "stretching" of muscle elicits a reflex contraction.

Figure 16.

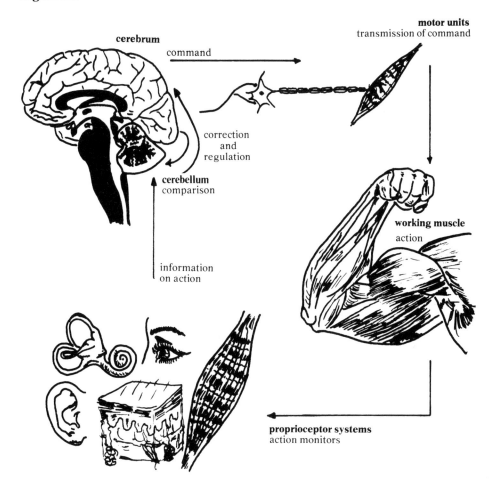

cerebrum

command

motor units
transmission of command

correction
and
regulation

cerebellum
comparison

working muscle
action

information
on action

proprioceptor systems
action monitors

27

Each athletic event requires a specific "expression of energy" in the form of *technique*. The role of each muscle group in a technique is referred to as its *auxotonic* role. For example, the auxotonic role of the back muscles in long jump is static, while that of the legs is a rapid exchange of yielding to, and overcoming of, the body's momentum. The coach must aim to develop in the athlete the most rational technique for a given event, ensuring that each muscle group is capable of performing its auxotonic role. At this point it becomes clear that the "production" of energy is closely linked with its "expression". The *conditioning* of the muscles to acquire and use energy is a basic requirement for technical development.

To summarise, the *central nervous system* controls the specific patterns of contraction and relaxation of the *muscular system*. Fuel from the *digestive system* and oxygen from the *respiratory system* are carried by blood pumped by the heart through the *oxygen transporting system* to the muscle, providing energy for contraction. It is the contraction of muscle and the resultant pull on the relevant parts of the *skeletal system* that provides the movements specific to given techniques. The body's *fluid systems* and *hormonal systems* are the major influences in ensuring stability of conditions within the body, so that the other systems may function efficiently.

ATHLETICS COACH

The Coaching Journal of the B.A.A.B.

Published: March, June, September, December

Details from B.A.A.B. Coaching Office,
Edgbaston House, 3 Duchess Place, Birmingham B16 8NM

Chapter 3

Woman and children first

(Special cases—Young and Female Athletes)

THE YOUNG ATHLETE

The coach must appreciate that, whereas the period leading up to and through adolescence used to be simply a preparation for serious competition in the athlete's early 20's, it is now also a period of preparation for high pressure competition within these years of growth. The climate of high pressure for immediate results can give rise to the extremely dangerous and ill-advised practice of subjecting the growing athlete to a biased programme of specialised training. Not all aspects of growth can be dealt with here, but the following may serve to illustrate the need for careful thought in planning training for the young athlete.

Anatomical Growth

With the exception of the skull and collarbones, all the bones in the body are formed from cartilage. The process starts from birth and concludes with the final ossification of the skeleton between 18–22 years. (Figure 17). Bone lengthens by growing at the junction of the main shaft and the "growing end" or *epiphysis*. The total process of skeletal growth is dictated hormonally, but is also influenced by the functional loading to which it is exposed. The hormonal effects of puberty make the epiphyses relatively vulnerable points in the body, and due to the fact that the bone material is not in its final mature form, the bones are more elastic, yet have less bending strength than in the adult skeleton. The effect on bone growth of *moderate* training is clearly positive. For example, the bones in a tennis player's racquet hand grow longer and stronger than those in his other hand. On the negative side, excessively biased loading may have a damaging effect, (e.g. Osgood-Schlatter's disease).

Figure 17.

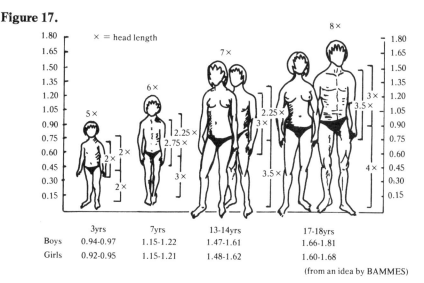

	3yrs	7yrs	13-14yrs	17-18yrs
Boys	0.94-0.97	1.15-1.22	1.47-1.61	1.66-1.81
Girls	0.92-0.95	1.15-1.21	1.48-1.62	1.60-1.68

(from an idea by BAMMES)

29

Physiological Growth

Due to the small size of the untrained child's heart, C.O. increase is brought about mainly by increased H.R. This frequency regulation, in contrast with the volume regulation of adults and trained youths, is a particular feature of the untrained youngster. Training increases S.V. and provides an increased range of functional ability by affording lower H.R. and S.V. at rest, and higher H.R. and S.V. under stress.

Muscle biochemistry in pre-puberty does not favour anaerobic activity. In repeated high intensity, incomplete recovery training then, the load placed on the circulo-respiratory system, and more specifically the heart, may suggest a training effect which is quite different in character to similar training in adults.

The peak of biological adaptability in children occurs between 10 and 15 years, at a time when physical capacity is far from approaching its maximum.

Training during adolescence will eventually increase the lung capacities. It was formerly believed that outstanding endurance fitness could only be acquired if specific training was commenced before puberty. However, endurance training of the aerobic type has a similar relative effect at all ages. Due to the existence of natural androgenic hormone to an extent never matched elsewhere in their life, girls should be exposed to regular moderate strength training as soon as they finish their adolescent growth spurt, but before sexual maturity.

Psycho-motor Growth

"The imitative capacity, freedom from social inhibitions and the irresistible urge to dominate the body in every possible (or impossible!) manner, endows the child between 8 and 10 with an almost immeasurable ability for motor learning." (SZMODIS)

(HARRE puts this critical period at 8–11 years (girls) and 8–13 years (boys).)

This capacity must be met with the best possible teaching, for never again will the child so readily master techniques. Due to the fact that bone growth always precedes muscle development, proprioceptive mechanisms lose their previous reference patterns through adolescence, causing problems of coordination through this phase of growth. This makes motor learning a lengthy and exhausting process and, when coupled with the fatiguing business of growth itself, implies longer recovery periods between training units and within training units. The coach should observe the young athlete closely in training and competition for signs of fast or excessive fatigue. Should these appear, the athlete should be asked to visit his G.P. for a check-up.

THE FEMALE ATHLETE

The reduction of male-female differences in performances (Table 4) might be attributed to greater female participation in the sport; improved training methods; and an understanding of male-female difference in basic characteristics of structure and function. This understanding has led to a more thoughtful application of coaching to the unique requirements of the female athlete. The most significant differences in these basic characteristics should be noted.

TABLE 4

Women's world records expressed as a % of men's world records in 1957, 1967, 1977, and 1987. Track events are generally close to 90%. Long Jump and High Jump are closing slowly towards 90% — which would require leaps of 8.01m and 2.18m. Comparisons are difficult in the throws due to different weights of implement.

EVENT	1957	1967	1974	1977	1987
100M	89.4	90.1		91.5	92.25
200M	88.8	88.1		89.2	90.83
400M	84.3	85.7		89.0	92.11
800M	84.6	86.1		90.0	89.82
1500M		83.3		89.9	90.08
3000M			85.5	89.7	89.91
10000M					90.03
400H			84.3	85.3	88.84
High Jump	81.9	83.8		85.8	86.36
Long Jump	78.1	81.0		78.5	83.71
Shot Putt	87.1	85.4		102.3	98.78
Discus	96.2	93.9		99.5	100.65
Javelin	64.7	68.0		73.3	75.29†
Marathon				83.1	90.13

† 90.07% (women v. men's new javelin)

Anatomical Differences

Women have narrower shoulders and broader hips than men. Different angles of tendon attachment to, and of muscle alignment with, bone reduces the efficiency of muscle pull and increases injury potential. The caucasian hip width difference is less than the negroid difference (10mm v 21mm), but this may be offset by a longer negroid leg—5mm on average for male and female.

The weight of a woman's brain is 92.5% and the heart 80% that of a man. The total time of pubescent growth lasts longer for boys, although girls start earlier by 1.5–2 years. The 14 year old girl is already approximately 97% final height and 96% final leg length at 18 years. On the other hand, 14 year old boys are approximately 85% final height and 80% final leg length at 18–21 years. Women normally enjoy a greater range of joint action than men, and their centre of gravity—due to a greater distribution of weight towards the hips/thighs and, on average, a shorter spine (86% of men's)—is lower than in men.

Physiological Differences

The general picture of the oxygen transporting system indicates that women's aerobic capacity is far below that of men.

Blood volume	60%
Red blood cells	89%
Haemoglobin	89%
Total lung capacity	61%

This situation alone could account for the male-female difference in endurance events.

31

Women do, however, have a greater natural store of fuel in the form of fat (156% compared with men—against body weight) and this may explain women's high performance capacity in the very long endurance events such as marathon.

There is virtually no difference between men and women in terms of anaerobic capacity. The same degree of acidosis may be tolerated by both sexes.

One very obvious male-female difference influencing the female lifestyle is the female *menstrual cycle*. Figure 18 provides a rough guide to the changes in efficiency capacity, where body weight is a factor, throughout the cycle. During the pre-menstrual phase (days 22–28), various salts accumulate in the body's tissues, encouraging the retention of fluid to maintain salt-water balance. This causes swelling in the lower abdomen and, in some instances, a visible weight gain around the tops of the thighs. The extent of this weight gain varies greatly, but is normally in the 0.5–3kg range. The athlete "feels heavy"; is vulnerable to injury and to infection; is more prone to emotional upset; may lose concentration more readily; and it has been suggested that the capacity of spatial judgement may decrease due to fluid pressure within the eyes.

Figure 18.

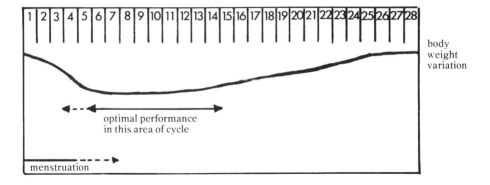

There is no evidence to support loss of performance capacity *during* menstruation. In fact, between 1956 and 1968, 21 Olympic Gold Medals were won during menstruation.

Menstruation calendars are used by many athletes (Figure 19) to plot regularity and extent of blood loss. This may be an appendix to the athlete's training diary.

It would appear that menstruation is occurring earlier now (13yrs 2 mths–13yrs 4mths) than in 1890 when 15 years was the age of menarche. It may be earlier or later.

It has been known for a girl athlete to become quite anaemic due to the monthly loss of blood and cumulative stress of her lifestyle. Only a doctor may diagnose this and treat it. However, should an athlete appear pale and fatigue quickly in training, the coach would be wise to suggest that the athlete visits her G.P. for a check-up.

Figure 19.
Menstruation calendar (adapted from JÄGER and OELSCHLÄGEL)

DAY		1	2	3	4	5	6	7	8	9	10	11.	12......
J A N U A R Y	blood loss												
	how you feel	3	1	2	2	1	1	1	1				
	weight	56	56	56	55.5	55.5	55.5	55.5	55.5	55.5	55.0		
F E B R A R A Y	blood loss												
	how you feel	2	2	3	2	1	1						
	weight	56.5	56	56	55.5	55.5	55.5	55.5	55				
M A R C H	blood loss												

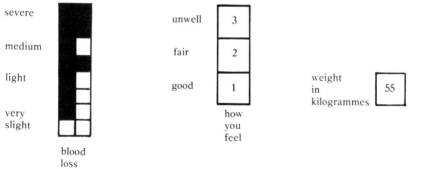

severe / medium / light / very slight — blood loss

unwell 3 / fair 2 / good 1 — how you feel

weight in kilogrammes — 55

Athletes returning to competition following pregnancy have continued to improve performance. The rate of improvement after pregnancy has been shown in most cases to be greater than the improvement rate before pregnancy, or the improvement rate of peer groups who have not been pregnant. (ZAHARIEVA).

Psycho-motor and Psychological Differences
The female athlete is approximately 7% more efficient than the male athlete in coordination abilities.

Recent thinking is that typically male or female behaviour characteristics are prescribed by society. However, differences *do* exist, whether imposed by society or inherited. These differences are difficult to quantify, but the most clearly identifiable are:—

Psychological stress brought on by competition is higher in women.
Women are much more dependent on personal care.
Women are much more readily motivated.
The fear of losing more readily replaces the hope of success.
Women are more difficult to coach in group situations than men.
Psychological patterns vary in the course of the menstrual cycle.

The coach, when planning training for young athletes and for female athletes, must understand the implications of those factors which identify them as unique groups. Table 5 is presented by way of summary of these implications.

TABLE 5
THE YOUNG ATHLETE

He should develop a sound basis of general strength, endurance and mobility before being introduced to technique.
He should be given the most knowledgeable coaching and teaching available for technical development, and have the opportunity to learn all athletics techniques before endeavouring to specialise.
The best ages for learning technique and for developing speed in joint actions are 8–11 (girls) and 8–13 (boys).
Training loads should progress through adolescence, but more recovery time should be allowed.
A balanced all-round programme of training is best for the growing child, reflecting varied loadings of all joint actions and energy producing systems.
Fast or excessive fatigue suggests that the young athlete should visit a G.P. for a check-up.

THE FEMALE ATHLETE
Strength training should be introduced in an organized way as soon as she finishes her adolescent growth spurt.
Strength training must be progressed more gently than for men.
Aerobic endurance training should be emphasised for the endurance athlete.
Training loads should be reduced in intensity from day 26 to day 1 (inclusive) of the menstrual cycle.
Relaxation training should be used to help create a basis for psychological stability.
Pallor and excessive fatigue suggest that the athlete checks with her G.P.

34

Chapter 4

Coming to Terms *(Terminology of Fitness)*

Fitness might be defined as the degree of adaptation to the stressors of a given lifestyle. Against the background of a fitness to tolerate the stressors of day to day living, the athlete seeks to acquire a fitness specific to the demands of an athletics event. It must be borne in mind that just as the demands of each athletics event are diverse, so also are the day-to-day lives of the athletes. If the athlete is "unfit" for life outside athletics due to an inability to adapt to its stressors, then there will certainly be an overlap into athletics and his capacity for developing athletics "fitness' will be impaired. "Management" has already been identified as one of the coach's roles with respect to the athlete's athletic life but, on occasion, wise counsel from coach to athlete may help "management" outside athletics, and consequently help the athlete in his pursuit of fitness within and without athletics.

A scientifically based and systemised programme of *training* is fundamental to the successful pursuit of high level athletic performance.

The athlete seeks a fitness that will help him gain competitive advantage in his event. Development of his fitness is based on a scientific and systemised programme of *training*. *Training Theory* is the interpretation of relevant work from those areas of knowledge which may provide the scientific and systemised programme against the backcloth of a growing volume of practical coaching experience. *Exercise* or *practice* is the principal training medium which, by varying its nature, quantity and quality, represents a broad spectrum of very specific stressors. The athlete's various systems, in *adapting* to these stressors, combine to make the athlete fitter to meet the demands of the given exercise. Analysis of a given athletic event provides the necessary information for selecting specific relevant stressors or types of exercise. These, organised within a training programme, develop the athlete's fitness relative to the demands of the event and consequently progress his pursuit of competitive advantage. The total process might be thought of as *progressive adaptation*.

TABLE 6
Examples of training units and objectives.

OBJECTIVE	UNIT
(i) Development of sprinting speed	$3 \times 6 \times 30$m rolling start sprints 4 mins between repetitions 7–10 mins between sets
(ii) Development of aerobic endurance	20km steady run. Heart Rate 145–155
(iii) Active recovery	20–30 mins squash

A diet of exercise may be organised into a single practice session in pursuit of a training objective. This single practice session is known as a *training unit*. (Table 6). The organisation of the diet of exercise may be such that a given practice is *repeated* several times; hence the expression *repetitions*. An athlete may, then, in a training unit, run 6 repetitions of 200m (6 × 200m). According to Finnish coaches "Repetition is the mother of learning" which suggests that the total number of technically sound repetitions of the quality required should be kept relatively high. In order to ensure that fatigue does not impair the technical precision or quality of a given exercise, high numbers of repetitions are divided into smaller groups, or *sets*. Thus, rather than attempt to perform 30 repetitions of "standing" throws (1 × 30), an athlete might perform 5 sets of 6 repetitions (5 × 6). Between repetitions, a period of *recovery* is inserted to maintain quality in each of the 6 repetitions in the set. Between sets, there is a longer period of recovery to ensure that the athlete is "fresh" for the next set. Normally these recoveries are stated as periods of time, but they may also be more tightly defined as an activity (e.g. *jog* 2 mins.).

Although the term "repetitions" is used in various types of training ranging from circuits to track work, it should be noted that the term *repetition training* normally refers only to running.

The nature of a training unit as a stressor, to which the athlete's functional capacity must adapt, is referred to as the *load* or *stimulus*. *Loading* produces fatigue, and cessation of loading is followed by *recovery* which returns the athlete not only to his original status, but above it. This "overshoot" phenomenon has been termed *overcompensation* or *super-compensation* by Yakovlev. (Figure 20). Yakovlev's representation of the training process symbolises two of the three "laws of training".

Figure 20.
Overcompensation curve (from YAKOVLEV)

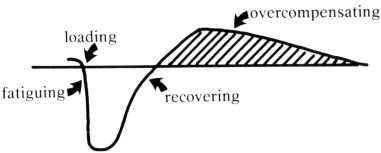

The first is the *law of overload*, which states that the nature of loading must challenge the athlete's present status. The overcompensation concept clearly illustrates how this is possible. Ideally, subsequent loadings should be introduced at the "peak" of over-compensation. (Figure 21a). To repeat a loading earlier or later in the cycle of events will not produce the same nett effect of progression. Or, in other words, the degree of overloading would be less than optimal, and this would be reflected in reduced effect. Exceptions here are those endurance training units where loading is to be introduced following *incomplete* recovery. (Figures 21b and c).

Figure 21.

Schematic representation of progressive overload. (from HARRE)

'a' based on overcompensation

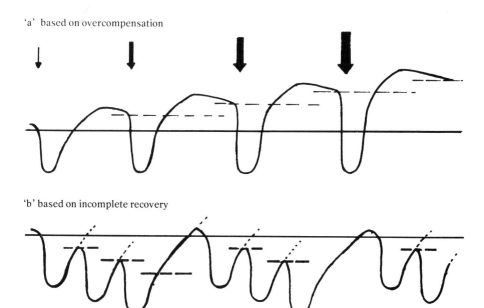

'b' based on incomplete recovery

The second is the *law of reversibility*, and this states quite simply that when there is no loading and consequently no need to adapt, the functional capacity of the athlete will return to a basic status consistent with the demands of his lifestyle. This is symbolised in Figure 20 by the downward slope of the overcompensation curve. Figure 22 illustrates the "reversibility" situation in strength training. The key to meeting these two laws is in the term *progressive overload*. The coach must, then, see loading and recovery as one total process, and establish for a given athlete the correct *training ratio* (load:recovery) within a training unit (intra-unit) and between training units (inter unit). The training ratio, then, will dictate optimal *frequency* of loading.

The third law of training referred to is the *law of specificity*, which states that the specific nature of a load will produce a specific training effect. The coach must consider specificity in terms of the athlete and his need to adapt to the demands of a specific event. The load assumes a specific characteristic by defining it in terms of the following:—

(a) *The training ratio*—which has already been discussed.
(b) *The structure of loading*—which is the relating of intensity to extent of loading in a training unit and within groups of training units.

The *intensity* is the strength of the stimulus, or the concentration of work executed per unit of time within a series of stimuli. Intensity may also be thought of as the *quality* of the training unit.

Figure 22.

Effect of weekly and daily strength training compared in terms of gain– and loss on cessation of training. (from HETTINGER)

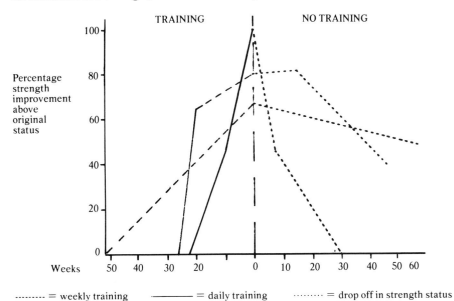

-------- = weekly training ———— = daily training ········ = drop off in strength status

Units of measurement of intensity for endurance or speed are expressed in metres/sec or frequency of movement (e.g. stride rate). For strength exercises, the amount of resistance is measured in kg or Joules; and for jumping or throwing, the height or distance, loaded or unloaded, is used. Frequently, "spheres of intensity" are referred to in sports literature. Table 7 is advanced as a guide to terminology in this area. Where such characteristics as maximum strength, elastic strength and speed are being developed, the highest possible intensity (or 100%) is taken as the best performance by the individual athlete in a given practice. For example, if an athlete's best 200m is 22.7sec., this would represent 100% intensity. If he runs 200m repetitions in training at 90% intensity, this would require a time of 25.3sec. for each run—and be referred to as sub-maximum training.

TABLE 7
Spheres of intensity

SCALE OF INTENSITY	% MAXIMUM INTENSITY
Maximum	95–100
Sub-maximum	85–94
High	75–84
Medium	65–74
Light	50–64
Low	30–49

38

In endurance events, *heart rate* is also used as an index of running intensity due to its close correlation with % maximal oxygen uptake. (Table 8). Thus coaches frequently refer to the intensity of a particular training unit by suggesting the range of *heart rate* for that unit.

The *extent* is the sum of all repetitions and/or their duration (time or distance) in a training unit. It is expressed in kg (the sum of loadings) in weight training; the number of repetitions in various types of training; and kilometres and/or hours in endurance training. The *duration* of the loading is the period of influence of a single stimulus. Thus for example, 20%–30% of maximum holding time is suggested as essential to the improvement of static strength. (GUNDLACH).

TABLE 8
Relationship of Heart Rate to % VO_2 max., against a suggested scale of intensity

SCALE OF INTENSITY	HEART RATE	%VO_2 MAX.
Maximum	190+	100
Sub-maximum	180–190	90
High	165	75
Light	150	60
Low	130	50

There is an inverse relationship between intensity and extent, and this has been interpreted by BUHRLE for strength training as in Figure 23. Because of the unique demands of a given structure of loading, it is clear that the training ratio will be specific to that structure and, of course, to an individual athlete. As a rule of thumb, the same structure of loading should not be repeated on successive days, except in the case of aerobic training.

Training units, broadly speaking, fall into three distinct categories, according to their contribution to the development of the athlete's fitness for his event.

Figure 23.
Relationship of intensity and extent of strength loadings (from BUHRLE)

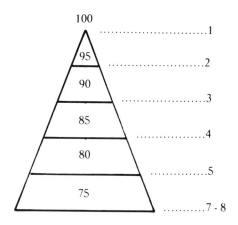

Figure 24.

Organization of circuit and stage training.

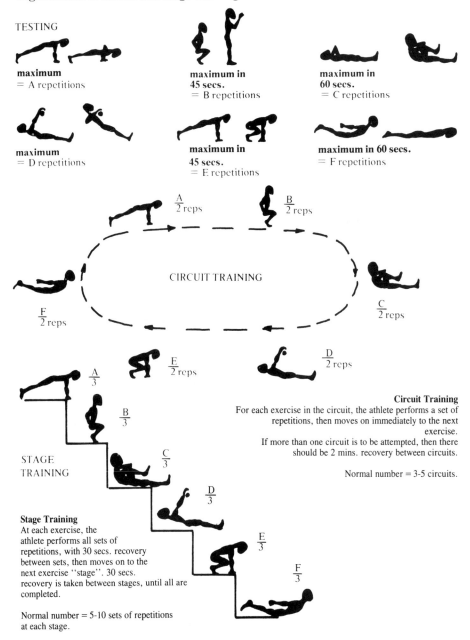

TESTING

maximum
= A repetitions

**maximum in
45 secs.**
= B repetitions

**maximum in
60 secs.**
= C repetitions

maximum
= D repetitions

**maximum in
45 secs.**
= E repetitions

maximum in 60 secs.
= F repetitions

$\frac{A}{2}$ reps

$\frac{B}{2}$ reps

CIRCUIT TRAINING

$\frac{F}{2}$ reps

$\frac{C}{2}$ reps

$\frac{E}{2}$ reps

$\frac{D}{2}$ reps

$\frac{A}{3}$

$\frac{B}{3}$

STAGE
TRAINING

$\frac{C}{3}$

$\frac{D}{3}$

$\frac{E}{3}$

$\frac{F}{3}$

Circuit Training
For each exercise in the circuit, the athlete performs a set of
repetitions, then moves on immediately to the next
exercise.
If more than one circuit is to be attempted, then there
should be 2 mins. recovery between circuits.

Normal number = 3-5 circuits.

Stage Training
At each exercise, the
athlete performs all sets of
repetitions, with 30 secs. recovery
between sets, then moves on to the
next exercise "stage". 30 secs.
recovery is taken between stages, until all are
completed.

Normal number = 5-10 sets of repetitions
at each stage.

GENERAL TRAINING

This is training for the general functioning capacity of the athlete. It is the foundation of endurance, strength and mobility through training units, ranging from the recreational (e.g. games such as basketball) to an ordered progressive plan of training (e.g. circuit training and stage training—Figure 24). The objective here is to ensure that the athlete will be fit to accept and benefit from special training.

SPECIAL TRAINING (SPECIFIC)

This is training to develop those characteristics of technique and conditioning specific to an event. Components of technique are isolated and developed via reproduction of the joint actions and the specific dynamics of movement associated with the event; while the efficiency of those energy systems associated with the demands of the event become the focus of concentration in the conditioning programme.

COMPETITION SPECIFIC TRAINING

This is training where technique and conditioning are completely rehearsed by applying the fitness acquired through special training to the event itself. More specifically, this is done in the competition situation. This area varies from a shade of special training to actual competitions.

All three categories of training are found throughout the training year, but the distribution of units of GENERAL : SPECIAL : COMPETITION SPECIFIC will vary according to the time of year.

The athlete's training year is seen as being divided into three *periods*, namely PREPARATION, COMPETITION and TRANSITION. These may be divided further into *phases*, described in broad terms by the training emphasis. (Table 9). Distribution of these phases and their location within the calendar year will be discussed in the final chapter.

TABLE 9

PERIOD	PHASE	DESCRIPTION
Preparation	1. (16–24 weeks)	General development
Preparation	2. (12–16 weeks)	Special development
Competition	3. (4–6 weeks)	Competition specific development
(Preparation)	4. (4–6 weeks)	Special competition preparation
Competition	5. (4–6 weeks)	Climax of competition season
Transition	6. (4–5 weeks)	Recuperation

Within each phase of the cyclic pattern of the athlete's years, there are other cyclic patterns. The *microcycle* is a group of training units organised in such a way that optimal value can be derived from each unit. More than this, however, the organisation creates a situation which allows each unit to contribute to the total character of the microcycle. The "schedules" planned by a coach to meet the athlete's training needs for a week, a fortnight and so on, may be thought of as synonymous with a microcycle.

41

The collective cyclic pattern of a microcycle, repeated several times in pursuit of a training objective, is known as a *macrocycle*; and the *phase* is a cyclic grouping of macrocycles. Certain literature also refers to *mesocycles*, which are seen as an intermediate step between *microcycles* and *macrocycles*.

The total structure of the training year may, then, be summarised as follows. To progress the athlete's pursuit of performance and/or competitive advantage *training units*, representing specific *structures of loading*, are organised for optimal effect by applying correct *training ratios* into *microcycles*. These are repeated with progressions to form *mesocycles*. The latter are again repeated with progressions to form *macrocycles*, the largest "units" of the *phase*. By the careful emphasis in distribution of general : special : competition specific training, the phases are planned to meet broad objectives relevant to progression through the three *periods* of transition, preparation and competition.

Chapter 5

Citius, Altius, Fortius *(Development of the Basic Characteristics)*

The specific fitness required to advance the athlete's performance and/or competitive advantage, relative to the demands of each athletics event, is developed by pursuing a unique pattern of training. This pattern is divided into CONDITIONING TRAINING and TECHNICAL TRAINING.

I. CONDITIONING TRAINING
This area of training is the development of the BASIC PHYSICAL CHARACTERISTICS. (Figure 25).

Figure 25.

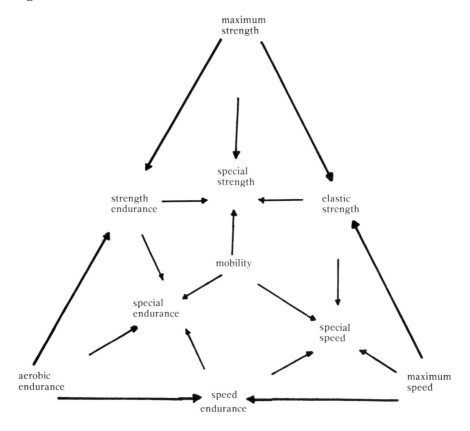

STRENGTH

The various classifications of strength are developed by the systematic use of *weight training* and/or *special resistance training*. (Figure 26).

Figure 26.

Both weight training and special resistance training are important ingredients of modern training. Both require supervision to ensure sound technique in pursuit of safety and efficiency.

Weight training is based on orthodox weight training techniques and equipment.

Special resistance training is based on the specific movements of athletics techniques, and equipment is drawn from many varied sources.

Maximal Strength

This is the greatest force that can be expressed by the contracting muscle. By definition this will involve neither speed nor endurance factors. Its contribution to athletic performance will, therefore, vary from event to event. (Figure 27). The loadings required for the development of maximum strength through weight training are suggested as $2 - 8 \times 1 - 5 \times 85\% - 100\%$.

Figure 27.
Role of maximum strength in various events.
(from HARRE)

weight lifting
hammer
shot
discus
javelin
pole vault
high jump (straddle)
triple jump
high jump (flop) —long jump
hurdles
sprints
800 —→ steeple
1500 —→ 5000
10,000 —→ marathon

44

Elastic Strength

This is that type of strength where both the contractile and the elastic components are assisted by reflex contraction in the expression of strength at speed. It is argued that it is relevant to all athletic events except those in the long endurance category—hence the adoption of hopping, bounding and jumping practices in the training programme of hurdlers, jumpers, throwers, sprinters and middle distance athletes. In weight training, suggested loadings are $2-5 \times 5-10 \times 70\% - 85\%$.

Strength Endurance

This is the expression of force in the climate of endurance factors, and is consequently most relevant for those athletics events where *lactic anaerobic endurance* is involved. However, because in training there is a demand for high numbers of repetitions in certain diets of exercise, it is recommended that *all* athletes develop a basic level of strength endurance. *Circuit training* and *stage training* provide such a basis for athletes in general, and this type of training normally precedes weight training in the annual training cycle. The loadings suggested for the development of strength endurance using weight training are $4-6 \times 25\% - 50\%$ max. $\times 30\% - 40\%$ for all events, and $3-5 \times 50\% - 75\%$ max. $\times 40\% - 60\%$ for those events with a high demand for this classification.

Absolute Strength

This is the athlete's maximum strength irrespective of his body weight. Thus the absolute strength of the shot putter in Table 10 is greater than that of the long jumper. Maximum strength development methods are applicable here.

Relative Strength

This is the athlete's maximum strength relative to his body weight. In Table 10, the long jumper's relative strength is greater than that of the shot putter. According to G.D.R. authorities this is best developed by loading the athlete, in the execution of whole or part technique, by not more than 5% body weight.

TABLE 10

Absolute v Relative Strength

ATHLETE	BODY WEIGHT	LEG PRESS FROM 90° KNEE	LEG PRESS / BODY WEIGHT
Female Long Jumper	56kg	180kg	3.21
Female Shot Putter	83kg	255kg	3.07

In this example, the shot putter has the greater absolute strength because she leg pressed the greater load; but the long jumper has the greater relative strength because she leg pressed a greater load relative to her body weight.

Dynamic Strength

This type of strength is required for those joint actions where there is movement in a given athletics technique. It is divided into *overcoming (concentric) strength* and *yielding (eccentric) strength*. For example, the former is required across the hip and knee joints in raising the weight in squat type exercises; while the latter is required in the controlled lowering of the weight. The loadings used for development of dynamic strength will vary according to requirement for maximum, elastic or endurance strength, and the need for absolute or relative strength. Dynamic strength should, however, be developed by dynamic methods (i.e. with appropriate movement) and not by static methods.

Static Strength
This is required for those joint actions where there is no movement in a given athletics technique—as, for example, in the hammer thrower's back in countering the pull of the hammer during the turns. Static strength should be developed using static (isometric) methods according to the nature of the static work involved. For example, the requirement for static strength in the back muscles is not the same in high jump and hammer throw.

Auxotonic Strength
This refers to the strength required for joint actions with respect to their specific role in a given technique. The detailed study of this role has brought about the many special exercises associated with different techniques. The nature of loadings will vary according to the demands for the various areas of strength already mentioned—but due to the importance of linking such exercises with precise technical movements, repetitions and sets are arranged to provide a high total number of repetitions without fatigue interfering with technique.

ENDURANCE
The various classifications of endurance are developed in several ways. Methods used include the scientific control of *training ratio* and *structure of loading* in running (Figure 28); *circuit* and *stage training; weight training;* and *special resistance training* such as hill runs, sand dune runs, surf running and so on.

Figure 28.
Summary of endurance training methods (from HARRE)

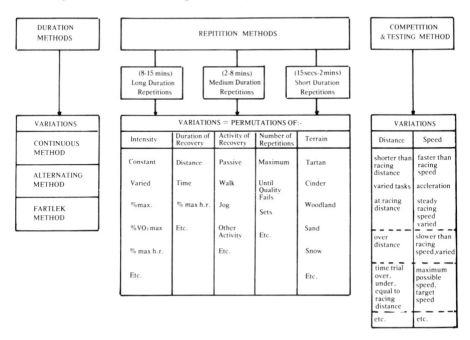

46

Aerobic Endurance

This is that type of endurance required where the nature of the event relies on the aerobic energy pathway. The longer the duration of the event, the more important this area of endurance becomes. It must be said, however, that a sound basis of aerobic endurance is fundamental to the development of fitness for all endurance events. It is possible to identify the following sub-divisions of aerobic endurance:—

SHORT AEROBIC	2mins —	8mins (lactic/aerobic)
MEDIUM AEROBIC	8mins —	30mins (mainly aerobic)
LONG AEROBIC	30mins +	(aerobic—fuel availability)

The most complex interpretation of training ratios and structures of loading is associated with short aerobic endurance because of the involvement of the lactic anaerobic energy pathway. STRAUZENBERG has emphasised the importance of ensuring that the duration of training runs is at least 2mins. if the biochemistry involved in this area of an endurance event is to be employed. It is possible to associate events with the areas of aerobic endurance. (Figure 29). Aerobic endurance is developed through duration training methods and the *interval training* method—a type of repetition training where the training effect occurs during the "interval" or recovery period between repetitions.

Figure 29.

Comparison and classification of endurance events according to short, medium and long duration.

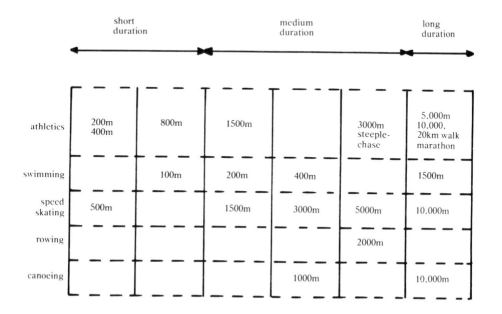

47

Anaerobic Endurance
This is that type of endurance required for those events where the anaerobic energy pathway is involved. It is possible to sub-divide anaerobic endurance as follows:—

SHORT ANAEROBIC	−25secs	(mainly alactic)
MEDIUM ANAEROBIC	25secs–60secs	(mainly lactic)
LONG ANAEROBIC	60secs–2mins	(lactic plus aerobic)

On a sound basis of aerobic endurance, this type of endurance is developed by using repetition methods of relatively high intensity and limited recovery. The exact structure of loading and training ratio will depend on the short-, medium-, long- anaerobic endurance aspect, together with the demand for *speed endurance* or *strength endurance*. Consequently, in addition to specific repetition training methods, special resistance training, circuit training, stage training, weight training and competition training methods are also used. Training for this type of endurance causes considerable wear and tear on the athlete's functioning capacity, and it is recommended that the practice of "hard unit—easy unit" on successive days be adopted, with this type of endurance training being considered as a "hard unit".

Speed Endurance
This type of endurance requires high quality speed of movement in the climate of endurance factors. In some ways it might be considered more an extension of technique and speed than of endurance, because the neuro-muscular system plays a major role. Repetition training methods are used, where sets and repetitions are organised in such a way that the required intensity of each repetition is maintained throughout the unit. This intensity is normally in excess of 85% max. By necessity, then, numbers of sets are high and repetitions within sets are low in number. (Distances run vary from 60%–120% racing distance). Relaxation is suggested as one of the most important factors involved, and practices such as "speed ball work" have been introduced to develop relaxation at a high speed of arm movement. Competition and time-trial methods of training are also used in development of speed endurance.

SPEED
Speed, as a factor in physical performance, refers to:—
   speed of coordinated joint actions, e.g. hurdler's lead leg.
   speed of whole body movement, e.g. sprinting speed.
   It may have a *direct* role in deciding performance, as in sprinting; or an *indirect* role, as in providing the kinetic energy to "compress the spring" of the long jumper's leg, or in providing high limb speed as in the discus or javelin thrower's arm.

Maximum Speed
Maximum speed of coordinated joint action may be developed by special *drills*. Although included here as part of conditioning training, these drills might be considered as a special form of technical training. They fall into two categories:—
   (i) Isolation of parts of a total technique, and the schooling of these parts at a speed faster than would be employed in the total technique (e.g. hurdles lead leg or trail leg drills).
   (ii) The schooling of total technique in conditions which permit a faster speed than would normally be employed (e.g. throwing with lighter implements, sprinting downhill or with wind, etc.).

48

Training for the development of speed is organised in such a way that neither endurance nor strength factors impair performance. Consequently, the duration of repetitions is always short; the number of repetitions in a set are few—although the number of sets may be high; and recovery must be long enough to recover from the previous repetition, but short enough to maintain neuro-muscular excitability. Distances used in training for improvement of maximum sprinting speed are 20–40m for young athletes and 45–60m for advanced.

Optimum Speed
The indirect role of speed requires the use of an *optimum* rather than a maximum speed. There are two basic reasons for this.

1. The athlete requires time to express his strength (for example, in the final pull on the hammer, for take-off in high jump) and to synchronise the coordination of joint action contribution and whole body movement (in throwing and pole vault).
2. When, for example, the triple jumper's take-off foot strikes the board, the total effect of his speed and weight must represent a kinetic energy which can be used to compress the "spring" represented by the jumping leg. Excessive speed will cause this leg to "buckle".

In these cases, the athlete requires not his maximum speed, but a speed suited to his level of conditioning and technique. The higher the athlete's maximum speed, the greater the range for establishing an optimum speed; and the greater the potential for performance improvement in all events *provided* the athlete can express his strength at increased speed. The development of technique and of strength are clearly critical here. The increase of optimum speed may be achieved by special technical work along the following lines:—

(i) Execute sound basic technique at a slow speed, (e.g. short approach javelin throw).

(ii) Execute this technique emphasising the *difference* in speeds of joint action, (e.g. same speed of approach as (i) but conscious acceleration of, say, leg-hip contribution).

(iii) Execute full technique at increasing speed, (e.g. extending to full approach).

Parallel to this progression must be the development of special conditioning work for elastic strength in the joint complexes involved.

Acceleration
The rate of increase of speed of joint action, or of whole body movement, is referred to as acceleration. Like speed, acceleration may be thought of as maximum or optimum. Maximum acceleration is required of a sprinter covering the first part of his race from the blocks. For him, there is a need to improve his speed of *reaction* to the gun, and to acquire the coordinated expression of strength at speed associated with achieving maximum speed in as short a time as possible. Practices here range from reaction training to technical development to the development of maximum and elastic strength.

Sets and repetitions must be given the same consideration as for maximum speed training—but distances used are 20m–40m for the beginner, and 35m–50m for the advanced athlete.

Optimum acceleration is required in all throws and jumps where optimum speeds are sought, or where there is a need for economy of energy expenditure (or tactical "bursts" or finishing speed) as in the middle-long distance races.

Having mentioned *reaction*, it should be noted that while improved speed of joint action will improve reaction time, the converse is not true.

By way of summary of strength, speed and endurance, figure 30 illustrates their relationship to each other.

Figure 30.
Relationship of speed, duration and strength of energy expression, as suggested by GUNDLACH

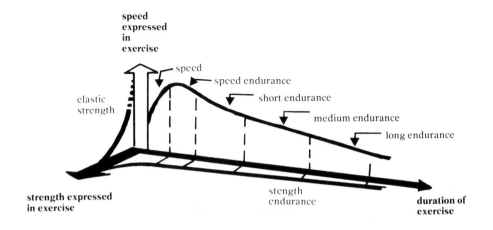

MOBILITY
Mobility is the range of movement of a particular joint action. In athletics, it is best to consider it as the range through which force can be efficiently applied—efficiently, that is, in terms of technique. There are three categories of mobility:—

Active Mobility
This is the range of movement possible by unassisted joint action. In other words, the athlete's own relevant muscle groups pull across a joint, stretching muscle ligament and connective tissue on the other side of the joint. (Figure 31a).

Passive Mobility
This is the range of movement possible with external assistance in the form of a partner, equipment and so on. (Figure 31b).

Kinetic Mobility
This is the range of movement possible due to the momentum of joint actions—as in high leg swings (hips). (Figure 31c).

50

Figure 31.
Mobility training is used to maintain or increase the range of joint action.

There are three types of mobility training.

a. ACTIVE

b. PASSIVE

c. KINETIC

The organisation of a mobility training unit should be:—
1. Raise body temperature by jogging, striding and general warm-up exercises in 1–2 tracksuits, preferably in a warm environment.
2. Active mobility and slow sustained work for each joint action.
3. Passive mobility with partners and apparatus.
4. Kinetic mobility.
5. Specific mobility combined with technique and strength.
6. Warm down.

Items 3, 4 and 5 must be supervised for the young athlete.

Training for mobility must not involve endurance factors.

II TECHNICAL TRAINING

Technical training is that part of the athlete's preparation which concerns the development of technique. The aims of technical training are:—

(i) To direct the athlete's learning and perfecting of the most efficient technique relative to a given event.

To meet this aim, the coach must have a complete understanding of the event and its technical demands; of the athlete's capabilities and their potential development; of techniques used by successful athletes in the event; of the related sciences upon which principles of structuring technique are founded; and of teaching and developmental methods. In short, the coach must establish for the athlete the most rational *technical* or *biomechanical model.*

(ii) To direct the athlete towards stability of performance of the learned techique.

This implies a progressive *opening* of the situation in which the athlete must perform the technique. Initially, the situation must be *closed*, affording the athlete perfect learning conditions, totally without distractions. Ultimately, in an *open* situation of bombardment by distracting agents such as weather, competition, noise and so on, the athlete must, within biological limits, be able to produce a technique as perfectly as in the closed situation. Moreover, this aim also implies the development of the athlete's ability fully to express his energies through technique in a competitive situation, producing a performance equal to, or better still surpassing those achieved in training.

Classification of Technique

Using DYATCHKOV's classification system, athletics techniques fall into two categories.

1. "Events where the aim of technique is to coordinate intensive strength of brief duration within the technical model demanded of the event." (Explosive and technical events: 100–400m, jumps, throws, vault, sprint hurdles).

2. "Events where the aim of technique is endurance development with an optimal expression of strength." (The endurance events: 400m, middle distance, steeplechase and long distance, 400m hurdles).

Again, referring to DYATCHKOV's classification, certain events also fall into a third category.

3. "Events where the aim of technique is the solution of those complex problems associated with interplay of athletes and/or environment."
(Events where tactical considerations influence the technical demands).

The athlete's technical development will be dependent upon the classification of technique.

Learning Stages

Broadly speaking, the athlete's learning of technique follows the pattern in Table 11.

TABLE 11

STAGE	DEVELOPMENT	TEACHING/COACHING METHOD & CONDITIONS
1.	First concept of movement is learned, followed by an attitude to its learning.	Previously acquired related knowledge plus general total concept of action influence this stage. Teaching objective is to produce an accurate basic action and eliminate unnecessary movements, etc. Demonstration and film accompanied by verbal instruction (simple) is indicated. Training must be concentrated, but too frequent repetition within a training unit will fatigue the beginner and impede learning.
2.	First ability to perform action and first acquisition of the action, i.e. the basic form of the action is performed.	
3.	Correction, refinement and differentiation. Finer coordination of movement.	Detailed learning of the movement is now worked on. Methods based on kinaesthesis (the feel of the movement) are used. Intervals between training units can now be increased, as can the number of repetitions within each unit.
4.	High degree of precision in performing the action in a "closed" situation.	Stabilise action and perfect technical detail. Training is designed to eliminate variables and give opportunity for "perfect" execution of the action.
5.	Precision in performing the action in an "open" (more variable) situation.	Progressive development of physical capacities (e.g. strength, elastic strength, speed, etc.) necessary for long-term development in performance.

Even with detailed planning and thoughtful teaching, it is possible for faults to arise. The exact cause or causes of faults must be accurately diagnosed, as it can often happen that the coach erroneously works on an effect rather than a cause. Possible causes are listed in Table 12. Correction may be pursued in a number of ways. For example:—

contrasting correct and faulty techniques via film, video, demonstration etc.;
guiding the correct action;
encouraging the athlete to exaggerate the action in terms of space or time;
working on an individual faulty *fundamental component*;
arranging that faulty performance is impossible;
practising the movement with the non-dominant side;
etc.

Correction is only complete when the athlete can clearly differentiate between correct and faulty technique in his execution of technique, and when correct technique is stabilised.

TABLE 12
Possible causes of faults

DURING LEARNING

misinterpretation of kinaesthesis and/or poor motor mobility

misunderstanding of concept of movement

negative interference from another technique

insufficient previous experience of components

interference of a poor learning environment, e.g. cold, poor equipment

premature introduction of strength and/or speed in technique

lack of physical abilities required by technique, e.g. strength, mobility

fear of injury

poor demonstration and/or explanation of technique

unpropitious timing of technique training relative to athlete's growth and maturation

etc.

WELL-ESTABLISHED

rational technique has not been learned

technique was not stabilised before competitions were introduced

athlete has known the fault but has lacked either guidance for correction or knowledge of the correct movement

due to poor status of physical abilities in learning, compensating movements have been introduced

the technique is incompatible with the athlete's physical structure of levers

coach has been lacking in knowledge as the athlete has progressed. (A technique which has brought success at a lower level may be inappropriate at a higher level)

poor training conditions

injury has caused compensatory movements

poorly organised training programme

etc.

Fundamental Components
It is possible to break down a technique into *fundamental components*, or the basic parts which are clearly identifiable as essential to the total technique. The establishment of exercises based on components demands a detailed knowledge of the technique of which the components are part. Each of these exercises must have the greatest possible range of application to technical development, yet further breakdown or modification of the exercise would be impossible without losing the character of the component. The exercises can be divided into two categories:

FIRST DEGREE DERIVATIVES are the exercises which coincide *exactly* with the essential parts of the component.

SECOND DEGREE DERIVATIVES are characterised by comprising only some of the essential parts of the component.

The basic technical model must be established before introducing second degree derivatives. There must be a constant relating of the part to the whole (total technique).

Technique training must not involve endurance factors *unless* the objective is to develop technical stability in fatigue.

Although each broad area of conditioning and technical training has been discussed separately, they must be considered collectively in their contribution to the athlete's specific fitness. Each athlete requires a specific blending of development in these areas relative to the demands of his event. The programming of this blend must ensure the progression of the athlete's status in each area with the least possible interference caused by development in other areas. In other words, the structures of loading and training ratios must take into account the collective loadings for development of strength, speed, endurance, mobility and technique to assure minimal compromise to their individual development, yet optimal effect in the athlete's pursuit of performance and/or competitive advantage.

The total training process might be viewed as in the schematic summary of Figure 32 — against a backcloth of the individual athlete's environmental variables.

Figure 32

SCHEMATIC SUMMARY OF TRAINING PROCESS TO BE VIEWED
AGAINST ENVIRONMENTAL VARIABLES

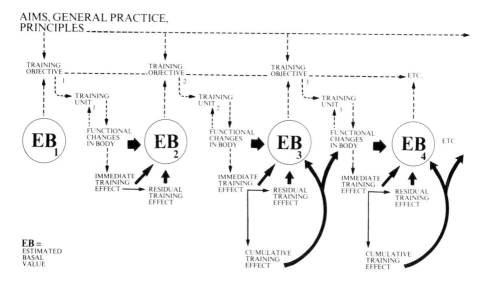

55

Chapter 6
The play's the thing . . .   (Planning the Athlete's Year)

The athlete's overall aim in athletics is pursuit of competitive advantage, and by meeting various short term objectives the athlete achieves this aim. Under normal circumstances, these are annual objectives which might be stated as:—
1. Preparation for an optimal improvement in performance.
2. Preparation for a definite competition climax.
3. Preparation for the main competitions associated with that climax.

Division of the training year to meet these objectives is referred to as PERIODISATION or the programming of units, microcycles, macrocycles, phases and periods to meet the requirements of both athlete and event.

Occasionally, annual objectives are not embraced by the three stated. These may be considered under two separate headings:—
4. Recovery from injury, illness or a particularly stressful training year.
5. Preparation for meeting objectives 1–3 in subsequent years by increasing special training status, stabilising technique/performance, and so on over the period of one or more years.

Special programmes are required to meet these objectives, and although they are not dealt with in detail here, the terminology and broad principles of programme construction still apply.

The periodised year might be represented as in figure 33a for an athlete preparing for a single competition period (outdoor season), or as in figure 33b for a double competition period (indoor season and outdoor season). These are respectively referred to as *single* and *double periodised years*. The distribution of phases/periods will shift according to the position of the competition climax in the calendar.

Figure 33a. Single Periodised Year.

months	Nov	Dec	Jan	Feb	Mar	Apr	May	Jun	Jul	Aug	Sep	Oct
phases	1				2		3		4		5	6
periods	preparation						competition					transition

Figure 33b. Double Periodised Year.

months	Nov	Dec	Jan	Feb	Mar	Apr	May	Jun	Jul	Aug	Sep	Oct
phases	1_1		2_1		3_1		1_2		2_2		3_2	4	5	6
periods	preparation				comp.		preparation				competition			transition

The phasing/periodising of the year against the months indicated is a suggestion for illustration. Commencement of the "year" will vary according to individual circumstances and requirements.

The year's training plan is crystallised at the conclusion of the previous season during the transition period. In putting the plan together, the coach requires certain information which will, of course, be interpreted in the light of current training theory. He must also be aware that within the framework of the constructed plan, he may have to make ready adjustment due to injury, illness, outside influences and so on. The information which the coach requires may be considered under seven headings.

(i) Knowledge of the programme of competition available to the athlete.
Even if this information is not available in detail, the coach must at least be able to fix the climax to the season; to insert "selection dates" (where applicable); and to plot the major competitions (indoor, cross country and outdoor) for the athlete against the climax and the selection dates. The climax to the season must be related to the athlete's performance status. Consequently, it must vary from athlete to athlete, and will range from the date of the Olympic final to that of a regional championship final, school championship and so on. When selection is involved in the athlete's progression towards the season's climax, the athlete must not view fulfilment of selection criteria as a climax, lest it become an end in itself. Pursuit of selection via performance in major competitions is part of a progression towards the climax.

The programme of competition available to the athlete may be drawn from several sources. For example, there are the international and U.K. fixture lists; the Regional, Northern Ireland, Scottish and Welsh fixture lists; the club fixture lists; and those of the Services and various student bodies. Not all will be applicable to the athlete—but those which are must be considered in terms of the athlete's progression through the season. (Figure 34).

Figure 34.

Possible distribution of competitions. Note that from approximately April 12th to May 31st there is almost a "grey" area where Phases II and III are bridged.

Date		Level	Event	Phase	II
April	5				
	12	(a)	200m; 110H; 4 × 100m (club trials)		
	19	(a)	Long; Triple; High (club trials)		
	26	(a)	Long; 100m; 4 × 400m (local club competition)		
May	3				
	10	(b)	Long; 100m (District Championship)		
	17	(a)	200H; 200m; (School competition)		
		(b)	100m; Long; (School competition)		
	24	(a)	100m (local club competition)		
	31	(c)	Long; 4 × 100m (Inter-District Competition)		
June	7				
	14	(a)	Long; 100m; 4 × 100m (Inter-School competition)	III	
	21	(d)	Long; 4 × 100m (Regional Championships)		
	28	(a)	100m (club relay trial)		
July	5	(c)	Long; 200m (Invitation competition)		
	12	(d)	Long; 4 × 100m (National Championships)		
		(a)	4 × 100m; 4 × 400m (Inter-Schools competition)		
	19				
	26	(b)	100m; 200m (club league competition)	IV	
August	2	(b)	Long (Open competition)		
	9				
	16				
	23	(d)	Long (Inter-Regional competition)	V	
	30				

(a) = Simple training competitions—low intensity
(b) = Build up competitions—progressive intensity
(c) = Main competitions—maximum intensity
(d) = Competition climaxes—maximum intensity

58

(ii) The planning of the year to accommodate the programme.
Once the basic competition programme is mapped out, the coach must divide the year into phases which will lead up to the climax. A decision at this point must be made on the use of a single or double periodised year.

According to MATVEYEV, the double periodised year offers a performance advantage for certain events (Table 13). It is not yet fully understood to what extent the double periodised year will influence the endurance events.

TABLE 13
Percentage annual improvement in performance comparing single and double periodisation

EVENT	DOUBLE PERIODISATION	SINGLE PERIODISATION
100m	1.55	0.96
Long Jump	1.46	1.35
High Jump	5.05	2.40
Shot Put	3.85	2.58
Discus	3.87	3.11

Given that the athlete has a stable technique, the double periodised year is particularly recommended:—
in a year where there must be a greater improvement in performance compared with other years;
where stability of competition performance is to be monitored as part of the athlete's technical progression;
where fitness status is to be evaluated relative to performance in the athlete's event during the preparation period.

For the athlete whose basic fitness is as yet incomplete and/or whose technique has not yet stabilised (mainly the young athlete, but also athletes who have changed events), the "extra" season should be seen as an adjunct to training or as a form of motivation. To break up the preparation period for such athletes, by specific preparation for competition, may exaggerate those faults which accompany the pursuit of immediate results, as opposed to an ultimate optimal improvement in performance.

Normally, neither the young nor the mature athlete should endeavour to pursue double periodisation for more than two successive years, because the basic reservoir of conditioning, which is the foundation of performance improvement, will be depleted by the physical and psychological wear and tear of full commitment to high intensity performance for what amounts to approximately 50% of the training year.

The phases of the year have already been described, and each has its own unique objectives and characteristic content.

Phase 1
Objectives

(i) Diagnosis of "hang-over" injuries or deficiencies from the competition season, and pursuit of any necessary therapy.
(ii) General development of endurance, strength and mobility.
(iii) Realignment of the basic technical model ("schooling").
(iv) Preparation for Phase 2.

Because of the distance away from the next competition period, it is tempting to structure this phase very loosely in the belief that all can be tightened up later. However, the entire year is founded on this phase, and each objective must be met.

Therapy may range from a revision of diet—which must continue far beyond this phase—to compensatory exercise, which must be completed before training for general development or realignment of the basic technical model may commence.

Phase 2
Objectives

(i) Progressive development of fitness specific to the demands of the event.
(ii) Development of the advanced technical model.
(iii) Preparation for Phase 3.

It is absolutely essential that the coach accurately evaluates the status of the athlete relative to the demands of the event, and to the type of training which such demands require. The coach should have a very thorough knowledge of special practices, and must exercise fine judgement in the balance of the structure of loading. This is certainly the most exacting phase of the year for the athlete in terms of loading. Winter ailments such as 'flu and colds contribute to the problems of planning for this phase.

Phase 3
Objectives

(i) Progressive intensity of competition experience.
(ii) Improvement of competition performance.
(iii) Technical evaluation of performance in the competition situation.
(iv) (under certain circumstances) Expansion of competition experience.
(v) (again, under certain circumstances) Gaining selection for the climax competition.

The total number of competitions to be attempted by an athlete, and their frequency in a season, will vary considerably according to event and stage of development. Young athletes are happy to compete whenever possible; very advanced athletes may tend to restrict the number of high intensity contests in a season to 10–12. If a double periodised year is used, the athlete will normally require fewer competitions to advance his "personal best" in the outdoor season than in a single periodised year.

The coach prepares the athlete for a given level of competition as the athlete progresses his competition performance. When the performance has stabilised, and only then, the athlete should be exposed to varying levels of competition under wide ranging conditions—even to the extent of injecting elements of surprise. It must be emphasised, however, that the performance must be stable, and that the coach is fully aware of the competition situation.

Evaluation of technical performance is critical here, because this phase represents the "dress rehearsal" for the climax of the season. The "qualifying" competitions may refer to meeting selection criteria, competing in preliminary rounds, and so on. The athlete must be thoroughly prepared to meet the challenge which these represent, as part of a progression towards Phase 5.

Phase 4

Objectives

(i) Realignment of the advanced technical model.
(ii) Preparation for the competition climax.

Phase 4 should represent a regrouping of forces for the final assault. Any fine adjustments to technique are now made, and a very specialised preparation programme is constructed. If "qualifying" has represented an exhausting struggle for the athlete, then the first part of this phase should emphasise active recovery and the promotion of a positive attitude to competition in Phase 5.

Phase 5

Objective

Achievement of an optimally high performance in the competition climax of the year.

A carefully structured programme of "warm up" competitions, together with short term cycles of preparation specific to the individual athlete, are important to the success of this phase. Errors here are more in the nature of demanding too much rather than too little in training. A post competition climax programme of competitions frequently reveals performances surpassing those up to this point in the season. A possible explanation for this lies in the fact that the athlete is under less pressure.

Phase 6

Objectives

(i) Active recovery from the competition season.
(ii) Preparation for Phase 1.

This phase should have as its main features a total removal of the athlete from athletics, and a vigorous programme of physical recreation involving very general activity introduced in its place.

(iii) The theoretical distribution of General: Special: Competition Specific training in each phase.

This will vary according to the athlete's event and level of development. Several interpretations have been suggested for establishing a pattern, most laying emphasis on a percentage of total training units in each phase. Table 14 advances such an interpretation based on work by OSOLIN and MARKOV.

From the table, it can be seen that just as there is a shift in emphasis from general to special/competition specific in the course of the athlete's year, there is also a similar shift of emphasis with progression of development over a number of years. The cyclical nature of this approach to training may also be reflected in the smaller cycles within the year.

TABLE 14

Suggested "training ratios" according to event and status of athlete. These are only guidelines and, of course, are open to considerable freedom of interpretation. However, they *do* provide a starting point from which a particular athlete might evolve.

BEGINNERS & DEVELOPING ATHLETES	I			II			III			IV			V			VI		
	G	S	C	G	S	C	G	S	C	G	S	C	G	S	C	G	S	C
(i) 10–14 yrs.	70	10	20	60	20	20	50	20	30	60	20	20	50	20	30	80	10	10
(ii) 15–17 yrs.	60	20	20	50	25	25	50	20	30	50	25	25	56	20	30	70	20	10
(iii) 18–19 yrs.	50	25	25	40	25	35	25	25	50	45	30	25	15	25	60	75	15	10
(iv) Novice Seniors	50	25	25	40	25	35	25	25	50	45	30	25	25	25	50	75	15	10

EXPERIENCED ATHLETES	I			II			III			IV			V			VI		
	G	S	C	G	S	C	G	S	C	G	S	C	G	S	C	G	S	C
(v) Sprints, Long and Triple	25	55	20	15	60	25	10	55	35	25	55	20	10	60	30	80	10	10
* (vi) Middle Distance and Walkers	20	75	5	20	70	10	10	70	20	10	85	5	10	80	10	55	40	5
* (vii) Long Distance and Marathon	10	85	5	10	85	5	5	90	5	10	85	5	5	90	5	45	50	5
(viii) Hurdles, High, Pole Vault	35	35	30	25	35	40	10	40	50	20	40	40	10	40	50	80	10	10
(ix) Throws	25	35	40	15	45	40	10	40	50	20	40	40	10	40	50	80	10	10

*These statistics are based on "complex method" endurance training, and it should be borne in mind that "Special" will include the athlete's aerobic endurance training. "General" will be mainly compensatory work for shoulder girdle, abdominals, etc. via mobility work, circuit training, strength work, etc.

Key:— Data represents % distribution of General (G), Special (S), and Competition Specific (C)
Training per Phase (I, II. . .)of the Athlete's Year.

(iv) The number of training units and the training environment available to the athlete.
Careful structuring of the athlete's day leaves a period free for possible use as a training time. (Figure 1). The coach, with his knowledge of the time and equipment/facilities implications for each type of training unit relevant to the athlete's specific requirements, is now in a position to calculate the total number of training units available per week. (Table 15). The greatest problem in this aspect of programming rests in the area of facilities and equipment. If specialist facilities and equipment are almost essential, but not readily available, a compromise has to be struck between occasional lengthy travel to a specialist centre, and the regular use of more local but non-specialist centres or even the general environment (e.g. woods, beach, etc.). If travel is involved, time has to be allocated for it, and this will have certain implications for training time and the number of training units possible on a given day. This area of planning must, then, be given very careful consideration. No time should ever be wasted in needless travel, so the coach must endeavour to remove the need for this by ensuring that local facilities and equipment may be adapted to meet the athlete's needs. The coach must have the capacity to be inventive in applying related areas of knowledge to creating a programme of practices which the athlete may do regularly in his non-specialist environment.

TABLE 15
The total number of possible training units that can be fitted into this athlete's week is 17

DAY	POSSIBLE UNITS
Sunday	3
Monday	2
Tuesday	2
Wednesday	3
Thursday	2
Friday	2
Saturday	3

(v) The relevant structures of loading and training ratios for development of the athlete's specific fitness to meet the objectives of the training year in his event.
It will be clear from previous discussion that the classification of training as General, Special and Competition Specific is not sufficient to establish structures of loading and training ratios for the athlete. The coach, armed with his knowledge of the total number of training units available, must consider the content of these broad areas of training against the demands of the event—and, of course, the status of the athlete. Table 16 provides a guide to the characteristic content of each broad area, and serves as a basis for considering the training ratios and structures of loading for athletes in the events indicated. By applying the changing emphasis of training areas set out in Table 5, a framework is now set for the introduction of relevant practices in the development of specific characteristics of fitness for the athlete in his event.

63

TABLE 16
Fitness characteristics per event.

EVENT	GENERAL	SPECIAL	COMPETITION SPECIFIC
Sprints and Relays	Aerobic endurance Strength endurance Mobility Maximum strength	Speed endurance Speed Elastic strength Special strength (relative) (Special endurance 200m–400m)	Sprint technique Start technique Time trials Baton speed technique
Hurdles	Aerobic endurance Strength endurance Mobility Maximum strength	Speed endurance Special mobility Speed Elastic strength Special Strength (relative) (Special endurance 200m–400m)	Hurdles technique Sprint technique Start technique (Stride patterns 400m) Time trials
Middle Distance	Aerobic endurance Strength endurance Mobility Maximum strength	Speed endurance Speed Elastic strength Special endurance (per distance)	Sprint technique Time trials Tactical trials
Steeplechase	Aerobic endurance Strength endurance Mobility Maximum strength	Speed endurance Speed Elastic strength Special mobility Special endurance	Hurdles technique + water jump technique Time trials Tactical trials
Long Distance	Aerobic endurance Strength endurance Mobility	Speed endurance Speed Elastic strength Special endurance (per distance)	Sprint technique Time trials Tactical trials
Walking	Aerobic endurance Strength endurance Mobility Maximum strength	Speed endurance Speed Special mobility Special endurance (per distance)	Walk technique Time trials Tactical trials
High Jump	Aerobic endurance Strength endurance Mobility Maximum strength	Speed Special mobility Elastic strength Special strength (jumping) Related events	High Jump take-off technique High Jump flight technique High Jump approach technique Sprint technique Trial competitions
Long Jump	Aerobic endurance Strength endurance Mobility Maximum strength	Speed endurance Speed Special Mobility Elastic strength Special strength (jumping) Related events	Long Jump take-off technique Long Jump flight technique Long Jump approach technique Sprint technique Trial competitions

Triple Jump	Aerobic endurance
	Strength endurance
	Mobility
	Maximum strength
	Special endurance
	  (jumping & running)
		Speed endurance
		Speed
		Special mobility
		Elastic strength
		Special strength (jumping)
		Related events
			Triple Jump take-off
			  technique (3 phases)
			Triple Jump flight
			  technique (3 phases)
			Triple Jump approach
			  technique
			Sprint technique
			Trial competitions

Pole Vault	Aerobic endurance
	Strength endurance
	Mobility
	Maximum strength
		Speed endurance
		Speed
		Special mobility
		Elastic strength
		Special strength
		  (i) relative—upper body
		    and trunk
		  (ii) jumping
			Pole Vault take-off
			  technique
			Pole Vault technique—
			  work on the pole
			Pole Vault technique—
			  work from/off the pole
			Pole Vault
			  approach/plant
			  technique
			Sprint technique
			Trial competitions

Shot Put	Aerobic endurance
	Strength endurance
	Mobility
	Maximum strength
		Speed
		Special mobility
		Elastic strength
		Special strength
		  (i) absolute
		  (ii) throwing
		Related events
			Shot technique—basic put
			Shot technique—entry
			  and shift/turn
			Trial competitions

Discus	Aerobic endurance
	Strength endurance
	Mobility
	Maximum strength
		Speed
		Special mobility
		Elastic strength
		Special strength
		  (i) absolute
		  (ii) throwing
		Related events
			Discus technique—basic
			  throw
			Discus technique—entry
			  and turn
			Trial competitions

Javelin	Aerobic endurance
	Strength endurance
	Mobility
	Maximum strength
	Special endurance
	  (jumping & running)
		Speed endurance
		Speed
		Special mobility
		Elastic strength
		Special strength
		  (i) jumping
		  (ii) throwing
		Related events
			Javelin technique—basic
			  throw
			Javelin technique—entry
			  and approach
			Trial competitions

Hammer	Aerobic endurance
	Strength endurance
	Mobility
	Maximum strength
		Speed
		Special mobility
		Elastic strength
		Special strength
		  (i) aerobic
		  (ii) throwing
		Related events
			Hammer technique—
			  basic throw
			Hammer technique—
			  turns
			Hammer technique—
			  swings
			Trial competitions

Heptathlon and Decathlon	Aerobic endurance
	Strength endurance
	Mobility
	Maximum strength
	Special endurance
	  (jumping & running)
		Speed endurance
		Special mobility
		Speed
		Elastic strength
		Special strength
		  (i) relative
		  (ii) jumping
		  (iii) throwing
			Individual techniques
			Time trials
			Trial competitions
			  (individual events and
			  groups of events)

Establishing an athlete's inter-unit training ratio is a very individual matter, especially in the light of the fact that several characteristics are being advanced at the same time. The coach must:—

(i) Ensure that the ratio is maintained by counting *rest* or *recovery* in the total scheme of training units. This is best done by building in a rest day or days within the microcycle. (Table 17).

(ii) Check at least once per month that the balance of training unit distribution is being maintained—not only in terms of General : Special : Competition Specific, but also in terms of maximum strength : speed : technique : etc. It can happen that the athlete loses a number of training units for different reasons, and this loss may leave a gap in one particular area of training.

TABLE 17
The 17 possible units available to the athlete (see Table 15) are reduced to meet a training ratio more suited to the athlete. While the athlete can sustain 2 units/day, this creates a cumulative fatigue. By making Tuesday and Friday rest days, a training ratio of 2.5:1 is possible—and this ensures maximum benefit from each unit.

DAY	TRAINING UNITS
Sunday	2
Monday	2
Tuesday	(2)—or active rest
Wednesday	2
Thursday	2
Friday	rest
Saturday	2

(vi) The principles of unit, microcycle, mesocycle and macrocycle construction, and their variations according to the phase of the training year.
The framework of a training unit is represented in Figure 35. Frequently, due to pressure of time, the unit assumes a more complex form, when the athlete attempts to work on two or more characteristics in the period of time at his disposal. In this case, the unit may look as in Figure 36. As a rule of thumb, when this situation presents itself the athlete should always work on "energy expression" training (e.g. emphasis on coordination and/or intensity—as in technical training, speed, elastic strength and maximum strength) *before* "energy production" training (i.e. emphasis on endurance—aerobic and anaerobic).

66

Figure 35.
Planning the single training unit.

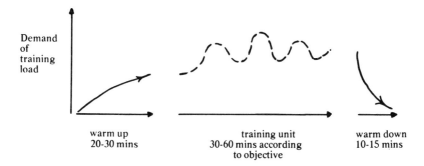

warm up 20-30 mins	training unit 30-60 mins according to objective	warm down 10-15 mins

Figure 36.
Planning the multiple training unit.

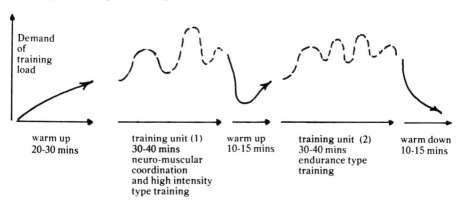

warm up 20-30 mins	training unit (1) 30-40 mins neuro-muscular coordination and high intensity type training	warm up 10-15 mins	training unit (2) 30-40 mins endurance type training	warm down 10-15 mins

Microcycles, and the larger mesocycles and macrocycles, are extremely varied in their detail. When studying these, it is more important to do so on the basis of "underlying principles" than at the level of detailed practices. The following interpretations of these principles are by no means the only approaches to microcycle-macrocycle construction, but they are offered as illustration.

(a) With the beginner athlete, it is usually the case that he trains 2–4 evenings per week. The general format is normally to divide each evening into a complex unit of (1) technical training, (2) conditioning training. Structuring the detail of a 1 week microcycle is not difficult because of the general nature of conditioning training, and the basic level of technical training. Nevertheless, the coach must see the total number of training units within a phase against the demands of this type of training, and prepare a programme over a number of microcycles. (Table 18).

TABLE 18
Planning development of the young athlete.

PHASE 1 — Week 1

	1	2	3	4	5	6
TUESDAY	(a) Sprint (b) Mobility and circuit (c) Repetition 100m	(a) High Jump (b) Mobility and circuit (c) Repetition 100m	(a) Javelin (b) Mobility and circuit (c) Repetition 100m	(a) Hurdles (b) Mobility and circuit (c) Repetition 100m	(a) Long Jump (b) Stage (c) Repetition 200m	(a) Discus (b) Stage (c) Repetition 200m
THURSDAY	(a) Sprint (b) Mobility and circuit (c) Repetition 150m	(a) High Jump (b) Mobility and circuit (c) Repetition 150m	(a) Javelin (b) Mobility and circuit (c) Repetition 150m	(a) Hurdles (b) Mobility and circuit (c) Repetition 150m	(a) Long Jump (b) Stage (c) Repetition 120m	(a) Discus (b) Stage (c) Repetition 120m
SATURDAY	(a_1) Sprint (a_2) General runs (b) Cross country	(a_1) High Jump (a_2) General jumps (b) Cross country	(a_1) Javelin (a_2) General throws (b) Cross country	(a_1) Hurdles (a_2) General runs (b) Cross country	(a_1) Long Jump (a_2) General jumps (b) Cross country	(a_1) Discus (a_2) General throws (b) Cross country

PHASE 2

	7	8	9	10	11	12
TUESDAY	(a) Middle Distance (b) Stage (c) Repetition 100m	(a) Triple Jump* (b) Stage (c) Repetition 200m	(a_1) Shot Put (b) Basic Weights (a_2) Relays	(a_1) Walk (b) Basic Weights (a_2) Relays	(a) Pole Vault* (b) Basic Weights (c) Relays	(a) Hammer* (b) Basic Weights (c) Relays
THURSDAY	(a) Middle Distance (b) Stage (c) Repetition 100m	(a) Triple Jump* (b) Stage (c) Repetition 120m	(a) Shot Put (b) Basic Weights (c) Special repetitions	(a) Walk (b) Basic Weights (c) Special repetitions	(a) Pole Vault* (b) Basic Weights (c) Special repetitions	(a) Hammer* (b) Basic Weights (c) Special repetitions
SATURDAY	(a_1) Sprint (a_2) Elected event (b) Special conditioning	(a_1) Triple Jump* (a_2) Elected event (b) Special conditioning *Long Jump for girls	(a_1) Shot Put (a_2) Elected event (b) Special conditioning	(a_1) Walk (a_2) Elected event (b) Special conditioning	(a_1) Pole Vault* (a_2) Elected event (b) Special conditioning *High Jump for girls	(a_1) Hammer* (a_2) Elected event (b) Special conditioning *Discus, Shot or Javelin for girls

Table 18. continued

In Phase 1, given a basis of general strength, mobility and endurance, the club athletes are given instruction in all events. Each training day sees a complex of 3 units: a technique unit (a, a_1, a_2) and two conditioning units (b, c). From week 6, the athlete may elect for an event for additional technical work on Saturdays, and with a growing knowledge of the athlete's status of fitness, the coach may devise special conditioning for the athlete—possibly related to his elected event. Relays are introduced in week 9 in terms of technical instruction, and then are used as a conditioning method. Mobility, once introduced, is absorbed in unit "warm-ups". From week 9, Thursday's repetitions unit is over a distance specific to the athlete's needs.

In Phase 2, the 3-day pattern shifts for 6 weeks to 2 days on elected events and conditioning related to athlete and elected event; and 1 day on continued technical instruction on the basis of week 1—elected track event; week 2—elected jump; week 3—elected throw, etc.—plus general conditioning. For the next 6 weeks, this pattern may be continued, or all 3 days may be devoted to the athlete's elected event and related conditioning.

(b) Convenience—and a basic preference for a microcycle that is built into normal weekly routine—produced the weekly type of microcycle, based on 6 days training and 1 day rest. The pattern continues throughout the year, with the rest day only altering its position in the week during the competition period. This microcycle is seen as a movement from general work on the first day (Sunday) to high intensity or quality work on the final day (Saturday). (Table 19a). Alternatively, the cycle may be presented as a programmed mixture of structures of loading, with the training ratio adjusted in such a way that one type of training acts as a form of active recovery from another, and the effects of conditioning training do not interfere with technical training. (Table 19b).

(c) One development of the 7-day cycle is to vary the detail of the week on alternate weeks. This requires the coach to establish a parity between training units and a developmental pattern for each area of fitness, so that at the end of say 28 days, pursuit of the training objectives of the phase are advanced on a broader front than would have been the case by using the one microcycle 4 times over. For purposes of illustrating the relationship of the various cycles, week 1 and 3 might be referred to as *microcycle 1*, week 2 and 4 as *microcycle 2*. Week 1 + week 2 may be referred to as a *mesocycle*, which is repeated to form a 4 week *macrocycle*. (Table 20).

(d) There are, of course, departures from the 6 + 1 day cycle, and the most significant variations here have been advanced on the basis of reflecting the year's broad pattern of preparation (Phase 1 and 4), adaptation (Phase 2 and 4), application (Phase 3 and 5) and recuperation (Phase 6) in the microcycle. The duration of the microcycle may vary from 7 to 21 days, with the longer cycles used in Phases 1 and 2, and the shorter cycles in Phases 3, 4,.5. The training ratio, expressed as training days : rest days, varies from athlete to athlete and, in some instances, within the microcycle. (Table 21).

69

(e) An extension to this approach has been used for endurance athletes who are following a training system which looks to be gaining the benefits of both the Lydiard method and the complex method. The duration of the microcycle may be 21–35 days and is founded on acceptance of the importance of a broad aerobic basis, while acknowledging the need to progress fitness specific to the endurance demands of the event. (Table 22). The cycle is repeated throughout the year, but there is a shifting of emphasis towards the specifics of adaptation and application.

TABLE 19a
One week microcycle moving from general to specific (Female—Long Jump).

Sunday	(a)	Stage training (8 × 60% max.)
	(b)	Fartlek—45 mins.
Monday	(a)	Weight training (3 × 5 × 85%)
	(b)	Basketball—30 mins.
Tuesday	(a)	Stage training (8 × 60% max.)
	(b)	2 × 4 × 300m (51 secs) (3–5 mins/10 mins.)
Wednesday	(a)	Weight training (5 × 85% : 10 × 65% : 5 × 85%)
	(b)	10–12 × 120m fast stride
Thursday	(a)	Technique simulation exercises
	(b)	3 × 3 × 150m (22 secs.) (2 mins/5 mins)
Friday		Rest
Saturday	(a)	Technique, off short approach
	(b)	6 × 20m rolling start : 6 × 40m standing start.

TABLE 19b
One week microcycle of mixed emphasis (Female—Long Jump).

Sunday	(a)	Weight training (3 × 5 × 85%)
	(b)	Basketball—45 mins.
Monday	(a)	Technique simulation exercises
	(b)	Specific strength training
Tuesday	(a)	Weight training (5 × 85% : 10 × 65% : 5 × 85%)
	(b)	6 × 200m (32 secs.) (3 mins, 2 mins, 1 min, 3 mins, 2 mins recovery)
Wednesday	(a)	rolling approach 20–30 × 9 stride
	(b)	3 × 4 × (30m sprint : 30m decelerate : 30m sprint)
Thursday	(a)	Stage training (8 × 60% max.)
	(b)	3 × 3 × 150m (22 secs) (2 mins/5 mins)
Friday		Rest
Saturday	(a)	4 × flat out runs to board
	(b)	10–12 × 13–15 stride jumps
	(c)	Specific strength training

TABLE 20
Alternating microcycles—to make a 28 day macrocycle of two repeated mesocycles. (Male—High Jump)

	WEEKS 1 and 3	**WEEKS 2 and 4**
Sunday	(a) Specific jumps strength training (outdoors) (b) Fartlek—30 mins.	(a) Surf running : bounding routines (b) Sand dune work with weighted jacket—30 mins.
Monday	(a) Weights $3 \times 5 \times 85\%$ max. (b) Basketball 30–40 mins	(a) Weights $5 \times 85\% : 10 \times 65\% : 5 \times 85\%$ (b) Basketball 30–40 mins
Tuesday	(a) Technique component isolation and special exercises (b) $2 \times 3 \times 300$m (54 secs) (3–5/10 min)	(a) Technique-component isolation and special exercises (b) $2 \times 4 \times 200$m (32.5 secs) (3 mins, 2 mins, 1 min/5 mins)
Wednesday	(a) Weights $4 \times 10 \times 55\%$ (b) Basketball/other game 30–40 mins	(a) Weights $3 \times 8 \times 60\%$ alternating with rebound exercises (b) Basketball/other game 30–40 mins
Thursday	(a) Specific jumps strength training (gym.) (b) $3 \times (150$–90–$150)$ (22.5/13) (2 mins/5 mins)	(a) Specific jumps strength training (gym.) (b) $3 \times (120$–90–$60)$ (17/13/9) (2 mins/5 mins)
Friday	Rest	Rest
Saturday	(a) Technique jumps—simulation + short approach (b) $2 \times 4 \times (20$m sprint—20m hold—20m sprint)	(a) Technique jumps—full approach (b) $2 \times 4 \times (30$m sprint : 30m decelerate : 30m sprint)

TABLE 21

21 day microcycle for a first year junior hurdler (male)—mid Phase 1. Times are included, as a guide, within which the athlete must maintain the quality of his runs. Technique must not, however, be sacrificed for speed.

PREPARATION

1. (a) Mobility
   (b) Basketball/squash, etc.—30 mins
2. (a) Technique—basic model
   (b) Stage training—6–8 × 60% max.
3. (a) Mobility
   (b) 2 × 4 × 60 sec runs (2 mins/5 mins)
4. (a) Technique—basic model
   (b) Stage training—6–8 × 60% max.
5. Rest (passive)
6. (a) Technique—basic model and drills
   (b) Weight training 3 × 8 × 70%
7. (a) Technique running and sprint drills
   (b) 2 × 8 × 30 secs runs (90 secs/5 mins)
8. (a) Technique—basic model and drills
   (b) Weight training 3 × 8 × 70%
9. Rest (passive)

ADAPTATION

10. (a) 6–10 × 150m hurdles (5–6 strides between)
    (b) Special strength exercises
11. (a) 2 × 4 × 150m (19.5–21) (2 mins/5 mins)
    (b) Weight training 3 × 10 × 60%
12. (a) Bounding routines and special strength exercises
    (b) 4 × 100 hurdles (i.e. 100 clearances)
13. Rest (active or passive)
14. (a) 6–10 × "broken hurdles"
    (b) Weight training 3 × 10 × 60%
15. (a) 3–4 × 250m (29–31) full recovery
    (b) Bounding routines and special strength exercises
16. (a) Sprint:—rolling 30m × 6 : block start 40m × 6
    (b) Hurdles drills
17. Rest (active or passive)

APPLICATION

18. (a) 10–16 × blocks start—2–3 hurdles—adjusted spacings for easy 3 strides
    (b) 3 × (120–90–60) (15.5/11.5/7) (2mins/5mins)
19. (a) "Clock sprints" 30m, 40m, 50m, 60m, 70m, 60m, 50m, 40m, 30m—full recovery between
20. (a) 10–16 blocks start, 2–3 hurdles—adjusted spacings for easy 3 strides
    (b) 100–200–300–200–100 (13/28/45 secs) (1, 2, 3, 2 mins recovery)

RECUPERATION

21. (a) Rest (active or passive)

72

TABLE 22
Possible 35 day macrocycle early Phase 2—for a female 1500m athlete.

1. 2 × 30 minutes*
2. 45 minutes*
3. 2 × 30 minutes*
4. 45 minutes*
5. 2 × 30 minutes*
6. Rest
7. 45 mins alternating (1km sections)† or cross country
8. 3 × 30 minutes*
9. 45 mins alternating (0.5km sections)† plus circuit or stage or special resistance training
10. 2 × 30 minutes*
11. 45 mins alternating (1km fast 0.5km easy)† plus circuit or stage or special weights
12. 2 × 30 minutes*
13. Rest
14. 45 minutes† or cross country
15. 3 × 30 minutes*
16. 45 mins fartlek with 10–12 long hill runs 200–300m (springy stride) plus circuit or stage or special resistance training
17. 2 × 30 minutes* finish with 10 × 100m fast
18. 45 mins fartlek with 10–12 × short hill runs 60–150m plus circuit or stage or special resistance training
19. 2 × 30 minutes* finish with 10 × 100m fast
20. Rest
21. Trial 5km on an even circuit but not on the track; plus 1 × 30 minutes*
22. 3 × 30 minutes*
23. 5 × 800m, track‡
24. 45 mins fartlek with 10–12 × long hill runs 200–300m (springy stride) plus stage or special resistance training
25. 2 × (600–400–300–200–100) track‡
26. 45 mins fartlek with 10–12 × short hill runs 60–150m plus circuit or stage or special resistance training
27. Rest
28. Trial 3 × 2km on an even circuit or track (*fixed* interval—10 minutes)
29. 2 × 30 minutes*
30. 2 × 3 × 500m track‡ plus circuit or stage or special resistance training
31. 2 × 30 minutes*
32. 2 × 5 × 300m track‡ plus circuits or stage or special resistance training
33. 2 × 30 minutes—finish with 10 × 100m fast
34. Rest
35. Trial—600m, 500m, 400m, 300m, 200m, 100m on track—*fixed* intervals 5, 4, 3, 2, 1 mins

* = H.R. 145–155
† = H.R. 145–155/160–180
‡ = pace and intervals according to athlete's progress

73

As the training year progresses, the pattern of the structure of loading assumes a characteristic form. (Figure 37). This form is reflected in the progression of structures of loading from microcycle to microcycle, and from macrocycle to macrocycle. (Table 23). It should be emphasised that the progression implied by the gradient of increase in intensity must be gentle in Phase 1. There are various ways of approaching the degree of progression. Some authorities advance loadings according to a fixed pre-set plan (Figure 38), while others decide the % increase on the basis of evaluation procedures at the end of each macrocycle.

Figure 37.

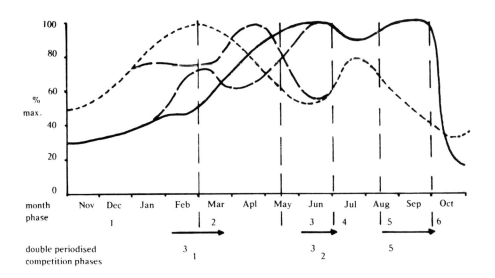

TABLE 23

DAY	WEEK 1	WEEK 2	WEEK 3	WEEK 4
Sunday	30km continuous	30km continuous	30km continuous	30km continuous
Monday	8 × 400m (62 secs) jog 400m*	10 × 400m (62 secs) jog 200m*	8 × 400m (62 secs) jog 100m*	10 × 400m (62 secs) jog 100m
Tuesday	15km alternating	15km alternating	15km alternating	15km alternating
Wednesday	4 × 800m (2:04) jog 800m*	5 × 800m (2:04) jog 400m*	4 × 800m (2:04) jog 100m*	5 × 800m (2:04) jog 100m*
Thursday	Fartlek—60 mins	Fartlek—60 mins	Fartlek—60 mins	Fartlek—60 mins
Friday	2 × 5 × 300m—jog 300*; jog 800m between sets	3 × 4 × 300m (46.5) jog 200m*; jog 800m* between sets	4 × 3 × 300m (46.5) jog 100* and jog 800m* between sets	5 × 3 × 300m (46.5) jog 200m* and jog 800m between sets
Saturday	Cross country/15km alternating/30km continuous			

This monthly cycle is repeated with increased speed of run in each unit where repetitions are used. The pace for this month is 62 secs/400m. Next month it will be 61 secs/400m. This is a microcycle based on the "Oregon System".

*Activity during recovery

75

Figure 38.
Interpretation of the "Lydiard Method" of planning endurance training.
(from SINKKONEN)

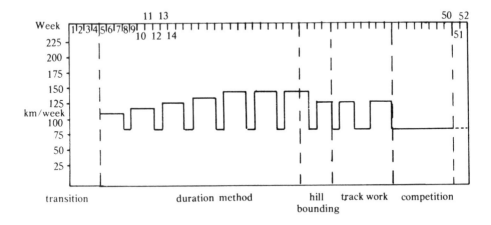

(*f*) Microcycles in the competition period are designed to achieve a compromise between advancing the athlete's fitness status and preparing him for competition. For the beginner and young athlete, this compromise will be effected by making technical adjustment the day after the previous competition—and by keeping the greatest training loads early in the weekly microcycle, while decreasing loads and increasing speed towards the next competition. (Table 24). If there is more than one week, then the situation is eased for the athlete and coach, with the possibility of a harder week of conditioning followed by an easier week of technical work, speed and relaxation. Not all authorities favour rest on the day prior to competition, but instead insert the pre-competition rest day two days before competition. In some instances, the day before now becomes a day of warm-up and mental preparation, while for others the training load is sufficiently exacting to introduce the possibility of overcompensation for the competition day. (Table 25). No matter which principles are applied in construction of the preparation microcycle, the athlete must arrive at the competition thoroughly prepared both physically and mentally. The most common error made by coaches in this phase is to work athletes too hard too late.

(*g*) The structure of the microcycle/macrocycle pattern of Phase 4 is dictated by the athlete's performance in Phase 3. Table 26 is offered as a guide to possible variations of approach.

TABLE 24
7 day pre-competition microcycle (Male Shot Putter).

Sunday   (*a*) Technique—component isolation and special practices
               (*b*) Weight training 3–5 × 3–5 × 90%–85% alternating with rebound exercises
Monday   (*a*) Technique—puts with varied weight implements (equal to or less than competition shot weight)
               (*b*) Special throws practices
Tuesday   (*a*) Basketball/volleyball/football tennis, etc.
               (*b*) Weight training—2–3 × 5–8 × 60%–70%—alternating with rebound exercises
Wednesday (*a*) 3–12 × "competition" puts
               (*b*) Special jumps practices/sprints/hurdles mobility, etc.
Thursday   (*a*) Basketball/volleyball/football tennis, etc.
               (*b*) Weight training 2–3 × 5–8 × 60%–70%
Friday   Rest
Saturday   Competition

TABLE 25
7 day microcycle prior to competition for an international level Triple Jumper. (KREER)

DAY 1   Sprinting: rolling start—full speed 20m × 5 repetitions 10 approach runs
            Weight training: mainly squat work with light weights—total = 2 tons

DAY 2   2–3 approach runs
            15–18 triple jumps (8–13 stride approach)
            Weight training: as for Day 1—but total = 2–3 tons

DAY 3   Total rest

DAY 4   Sprinting: rolling start—full speed 20m × 5 repetitions
            Hopping: 4 × 50m
            Sprinting: 1 × 80m
            Weight training: as for Day 1—but total = 4–5 tons

DAY 5   Total rest

DAY 6   Easy workout:—
            Sprinting: 2 × 50m, 3 × 100m
            Weight training: as for Day 1—total = 2 tons

DAY 7   Competition

TABLE 26

PREVIOUS COMPETITION SERIES	PROCEDURE IN SPECIAL PREPARATION
Performance steadily improved. Capacity for loading high.	Previous training microcycles continued, but re-charging emphasised in first week. Moreover, extent of lower intensity training raised for first 2–3 weeks, then high intensity of competition specific loadings in final 2–3 weeks.
Not daily training, perhaps every other day or 2:1:3:1 etc., but very high intensity of loading in each unit. Performances reasonable but small increases.	Move to daily training at lower intensity. Extent is, therefore, high in general and special but competition specific trainings should be low. Intensity is reduced for 2–3 weeks—then accelerated to very high—perhaps even returning to training every other day in last 2 weeks.
High competition frequency has interfered with total extent of training and normal progression. Perhaps no further improvements in performance, loadings of very high intensity.	Increase extent of general and special, but very low competition specific. Loadings roughly equal to late Phase II. Include 2–3 build-up competitions in last 2 weeks, i.e. highest intensity of competition specific loadings. This accompanied by all round increase in intensity, decrease in extent.
Poor or even regressive results of competition. Competition life is a struggle, yet training similar to last year.	Check with bio-profile and physiotherapist. If this gives the athlete an "all-clear":—

(i) *Experienced athlete:* Great increase in extent of all loadings 2 weeks; then great increase in intensity as extent falls for 10–14 days; then high intensity competition specific over final week. 1–2 build-up competitions in final 10 days.

(ii) *Inexperienced athlete:* Raise extent of general and special loadings for 2 weeks to values of late Phase II; 2 build-up competitions in successive days 7 days prior to major competition—then high intensity competition specific final week. If athletes are found unfit by the check-up, then the value of proceeding to the major competition is in doubt.

continued on page 79.

continued from page 78.

Early performances excellent—then "over-stress" symptoms appear as performances fall.

If this "over-stress" is traced to the nature of loadings, the immediate objective is to restore stability of training status. High extent of general and physical recreation activities, with rising extent of special training in first 7–10 days. Once enthusiasm for more intensive loadings returns, hold medium extent of all loadings with gradually raised intensity for next 10–14 days—then inject a steep increase in intensity, especially in competition specific, up to competition. Value of build-up competition is limited. If "over-stress" is due to other factors, trace source; then proceed as above.

(vii) The status of the athlete relative to the demands of the event.

Because the training situation is dynamic, knowledge of the athlete's status must be constantly updated to adjust units, microcycles and so on to meet the requirements of the athlete's present status throughout the year. The total evaluation process must, then, be a continuous revaluation and realignment of programme. (Figure 39).

The criteria which must be measured in evaluating the athlete's status might be classified as in Table 27.

Figure 39.

EVALUATE DEMANDS OF EVENT

EVALUATE STATUS OF ATHLETE RELATIVE TO THESE DEMANDS

DEFINE OBJECTIVES OF TRAINING

CONSTRUCT TRAINING PROGRAMME

EXECUTE TRAINING PROGRAMME

EVALUATE STATUS OF ATHLETE RELATIVE TO TRAINING OBJECTIVES

RE-DEFINE OBJECTIVES OF TRAINING

TABLE 27
Classification of factors in evaluation of the athlete.

GENERAL FACTORS	EXAMPLE
Anthropometric measures	Height, lean body mass, etc.
Physical capacities	Strength, mobility, etc.
Physiological capacities	VO_2max, haemoglobin concentration, etc.
Psychological capacities	Personality, etc.
Technical abilities (neuro-motor)	Motor ability, reaction time, etc.

SPECIFIC FACTORS	
Event performance	Personal bests, time trials, etc.
Tactical abilities	Tactical solution to specific situations, etc.
Technical performance	Technical analysis via video tape, etc.
General factors in specific events	E.C.G. during a trial, etc.

ENVIRONMENTAL FACTORS	
Finance	Requirements for travel, entry, etc.
Nutrition	Diet analysis, calorie intake, etc.
Occupation	Energy cost, study time, etc.
Social	Religion, social attitudes, etc.
Support	Physiotherapy, sports medicine, etc.
Training	Equipment, facilities, etc.

The results of this measurement and testing are evaluated by:—

(i) Comparing results with those recorded by the athlete in the same tests previously.

(ii) Comparing results with relevant norms or standards.

(iii) Comparing results with those of other athletes.

The evaluation may then be applied in pursuit of one or several of the following objectives:—

1. **To assess the athlete's aptitude for a given event**
   The most important condition for diagnosing aptitude is regular participation in the event, and a reasonable guide might be derived from the collective evaluation of the following:—

   (i) The status of the athlete's performance in the event, with respect to existing norms of progression according to age, sex, etc.

   (ii) The athlete's status in those capacities characteristic of the event (physiological, physical, anthropometric, etc.).

   (iii) The speed at which the athlete improves performance during the period of instruction.

   (iv) The ability to reproduce technically sound performance consistently (stability).

80

2. To plan the athlete's developmental programme.
This objective is met by applying, directly or indirectly, the data obtained from evaluating the athlete's status in pursuit of six "sub-objectives".

(i) To assess the effect of training systems on performance.
(ii) To assess the efficacy of training systems in developing status in event-related parameters.
(iii) To establish homogenous groupings for training.
(iv) To establish the characteristics of fitness demanded by a given event.
(v) To establish norms of structure, function and progression according to age and sex.
(vi) To assess knowledge of the event.

In short, evaluation procedures assist the coach to understand the athlete's training status and its development, and to make training programmes more effective in meeting the athlete's aim in pursuing competitive advantage.

There can be little doubt that the most valuable material to be evaluated in planning the athlete's programme is the content of his training diary. The B.A.A.B. Training Diary has been designed with this in mind, with special pages for information on: —

(i) Previous personal records.
(ii) Previous results in Fitness or Control Tests.
(iii) The planned competition programme.
(iv) An overall year plan (Figure 40).
(v) The training phases (Figure 41).
(vi) The details of microcycle content in each phase (Figure 42).
(vii) The day to day record of the athlete's training.
(viii) The season's competition performances and results.
(ix) A weight chart.
(x) A menstruation chart (see Figure 19).
(xi) A record of illnesses and/or injuries.
(xii) Results in Fitness or Control Tests.

The principles involved in planning the training year, and the various examples used in this chapter to illustrate implementation of these principles, should be seen as a reference structure. The complex of athlete, coach and situation suggests such an immense permutation of variables, that the coach *must* work towards a unique interpretation of principles at all times. This interpretation will be represented by a modification of the reference structure, and by a rich detail of training practice drawn from his understanding of the expanding field of training theory and from his growing experience of practical coaching.

This booklet has been put together with the object of introducing the coach to training theory. It is by no means an exhaustive work in this field, but it may hopefully encourage the coach to extend his knowledge in this area. Coaching is, however, a *practical* art, and in developing his knowledge of training theory the coach must constantly relate what he learns to practical work with an athlete, if he is to advance the athlete's pursuit of competitive advantage.

Figure 40.

YEAR PLAN

MONTH –WEEK COMNCNG WEEK IN TRAINING YEAR	1	2	3	4	5	6	7	8	9	10	11	12	13	14	15	16	17	18	19	20	21	▶
PHASE 1																						
PHASE 2																						
PHASE 3																						
PHASE 4																						
PHASE 5																						
PHASE 6																						
PHASE 7																						
PHASE 8																						
PHASE 9																						
PHASE 10																						
MAJOR COMPETITIONS																						
MINOR COMPETITIONS																						
MEDICAL CONTROL																						
TRAINING CONTROL																						
TRAINING CAMPS																						

NOTES

Figure 41.

TRAINING PHASES

PHASE	STARTING DATE	DESCRIPTION
1		
2		

TRAINING PHASES

OBJECTIVES

82

Figure 42.

MICROCYCLE

PHASE

1			
2			
3			
4			
5			
6			
7			

WEEKLY DETAILS AND PROGRESSIONS

TRAINING UNIT & EXERCISES	WEEK 1	WEEK 2	WEEK 3	WEEK 4	WEEK 5	WEEK 6	WEEK 7	WEEK 8	WEEK 9	WEEK 10

Bibliography

BOOKS
Leichtathletik, G. Schmolinsky, Sportverlag Berlin 1974 (7)
Trainingslehre, Dr. D. Harre, Sportverlag Berlin 1973
Kleine Trainingslehre, K. Jäger and G. Oelschlägel, Sportverlag Berlin 1974 (2)
Kestävyys, Valmennus, L. Seppänen and E. Oikarinen, S.V.U.L. Helsinki 1976
Periodisation of Sports Training, L. P. Matveyev, Fiskultura i Sport, Moscow 1965
Kinesiology and Applied Anatomy, P. J. Rasch and R. K. Burke, Lea and Faber, Pa.1968 (3)
Textbook of Work Physiology, P. O. Åstrand and K. Rodahl, McGraw Hill, N.Y. 1970
Biochemistry of Sport, N. N. Yakovlev, Leipzig 1967
Psychology and the Superior Athlete, M. Vanek and B. J. Cratty, McMillan, London 1970
Report on International Congress on Sports Injuries, S.V.U.L. Helsinki 1977

PAPERS
Training Theory (1, 2, 3, 4,), F. W. Dick, Loughborough Summer School, 1977
The Sportsman's Diet, M. A. Nimmo, Lothian Regional Council Lectures, 1977
Exercises and Their Selection, T. Craig, Lothian Regional Council Lectures, 1977
Training and the Growing Child, F. W. Dick, M.C.A.A.A. Coaches' Conference, 1977
Cardiovascular Adaptations to Physical Training, J. Scheuer and C. M. Tipton, Ann. Rev. Physiol, 39: 221–251, 1977
Psychology of Preparation for Competition, M. Vanek, International Coaches Convention Report, 1975
Introduction to Training Theory, F. W. Dick, Athletics Weekly, 1975
Training Stresses on the Growing Child, Dr. I. Szmodis, International Coaches Convention Report, 1976
Male-Female Differences in Training and Competition, P. Wagner, International Coaches Convention Report, 1976
Sport and Physical Education, J. MacDonald, International Coaches Convention Report, 1977
Microcycles Revisited, A. Ewen and F. W. Dick, International Coaches Convention Report, 1977
Competition Preparation in High Jump, E. Drechsler, International Coaches Convention Report, 1977
Thoughts about the Frustrations of an Athlete, C. Garpenborg, International Coaches Convention Report, 1977